A WORLD
—— WITHIN ——
A WORLD

E D W A R D   J O H N S O N

PAGE PUBLISHING, INC.
Conneaut Lake, PA

First originally published by Page Publishing 2021

ISBN 978-1-6624-1719-1 (pbk)
ISBN 978-1-6624-1720-7 (digital)

Printed in the United States of America

When I was five years old, I was beat up, robbed, and dragged through life without any say so. So now that I'm a man and older, let me share my pain with you if I may.

I was beat up by my sisters, mom, stepdad, and brother. Troy used to hit me with broomsticks, shoes, belts, anything. Lisa used to smack me in the face and say mean things to me. Tammi used to punch me and kick me all day long. Whenever they misplaced something, they didn't have to look for it. When they were watching TV, my mom made me sit right in the same room but with my back to the TV. Most of the time it was because one of them had told a lie on me, or my mom got mad about something she did. She would say, "Turn your black ass around, you don't need to watch TV.

Now when I say I was beat up, I mean they kicked me, punched me in the face, threw shoes at me, and said, I hate you, why are you here, we don't care about you?. I was told, and they would often say mean and hurtful things to me. Now when I said I was, I mean, what to do, where to sit, what to wear (no childhood or freedom). My bedroom was small, cold, and damp, with one or two small square windows. I never knew why but it was. Why they would make me sleep like that (broken windows, going to bed with a dirty body) I had a mattress that I laid on the floor by the window away from the door. I did this because if someone came in (sometimes I put my mattress against the door to stop mom), they would hit me with the door. To cover the mattress, I had a dirty white sheet with no pillow and no blanket. Sometimes my mom wouldn't let me come out of my room, not even for dinner. It would be days before I ate or got to go to the bathroom. I hated that because sometimes I would have to take a dump or pee in my room, and it stank. Then my mom would smell it and come in and beat me and rub it on my face, hands, or body. Now don't sit there and think that this isn't true because every word is. I got whooped with leg tables, bats, metal bars, and boots. My mom just beat me until I passed out or bled real bad, while calling me bad names. Names that children should not hear. As I cried, I used to see my sisters laughing and shaking their heads. Now there were times that I could come out, but first I had to do something like clean up all the clothes, shoes, or whatever because Tammy, Tom, Tracy would be playing in there, or my mom wanted me to get some money or borrow from somebody or look for her boyfriend, Sam.

I could almost tell what she wanted when she opened my bedroom door. If she came in hitting me, that meant she was drunk, or one of my sisters or brother lied on me. Or if she opened the door and said "Come here," that meant clean up to go somewhere or help her. Or it meant I could get something to eat, just not the same food everybody else had been eating. Now there were times when she would be in a good mood and let me come out and watch TV or eat. I never ate at the table, always on the floor. My mom and sisters said, "He smells like poop or he stinks." So I wasn't allowed to say anything or do anything to my brothers or sisters because they would tell on me, and I would get the shit beat out of me. So they told lies on me every day, all day long. Holidays were okay if you got anything. I would be allowed to play with Troy's stuff but only after he broke it and then lied on me. I never had new clothes or shoes. I never knew what school was like because my mom kept me home to clean the house or walk to the store. Or it was too late to go because I had to look for my brother's and sisters' stuff for school. If I was really bad like stealing something or sneaking out of the house to ask somebody for food or money, she would put my hand on the burner or knock me upside my head and hit me (with something sharp). I never knew how to play outside with kids because my mom wouldn't let me. She bought swing sets, but I wasn't allowed to play on them (it was for my sister and brother). They said that I was bad luck and would break it. Only time I got to play is when I went to school. I would first run to the swings, I was always I was so busy looking for food or money most times in school because I was hungry. If I gave my mom money, she would feed me, be nice to me, or let me watch TV. But I would eventually get sent to my room. I would come home from school, and she would say, "Sit in your room, I don't want to see your face." To Her it was just my room, but to me it was a cage where a dog sleeps. With dirty windows and no curtains, cold and damp, my room always smelled like pee with a dirty mattress. Dirty white walls with shit on them from when I got mad or if I couldn't hold it in because I wasn't allowed to go to the bathroom. I hated that room. It was always dark, cold, and scary. Sometimes I would lay there with tears coming down my face, thinking about me and my mom. I really don't know how or what my mom really felt about me. There was a time she would say something nice, and there would be times where she would show how much she could hate a kid. Her first son. But there were some good times. I was only four or five I would say to myself, is mom okay, I thought, she would give me candy. When I turned six, that was when my mom said, "Now you do this, do that, don't tell this, keep out the way." Whatever happens, tell them you fell." She didn't want people to know she was making me steal, lie, and take money out of mailboxes. That was my idea, then I told her. Sometimes, I didn't want to steal or lie, but I would hear my mom's voice: "You're a thief, and people hate you because you're a thief." So she would say don't tell, don't get caught.

It was a hot day, and I just knew I would be allowed to go outside and play. I thought to myself, I can go over someone's house and get something to eat. It was a Friday afternoon; my sisters got out of school and were outside playing, and I got on the swing set. I told Troy, my brother, that I wasn't getting off, so he picked up a brick and hit me with it. Then he ran into the house and told on me. I could hear my Mom coming and saying, "Adam, get your bad-luck ass in here." As I was slowly getting off the swing, looking down at the ground, thinking to myself, *I hate her and I'm going to get him one day.* I walked across the yard. I could feel my mom standing there ready to hit me. I was too afraid to look up, knowing that something was about to happen. When I finally did, I could see my little brother, Troy, standing there, smiling at me. I tried to think how I was going to get past her without getting hit, but I was too afraid to think. I thought to myself, "Run and run fast past her." As I ran, not thinking about anything, I fell right in front of my mom, the beater. When I looked up I saw my mom's foot, one blow to the head and one to the butt. "Get your ass in your room, you dumb motherfucker."

I got up crying and running, so afraid that she was behind me. I ran to my room. I knew that if I made it to my room I'd be safe. I would lay on my dirty, wet, pee mattress curled up in a ball, crying and holding myself, too afraid to cry out loud. Mom would be drunk sometimes and come into the room and kick me and spit on me. She would call me bad names and tell me how much she hated my dad and me because I look like him. As I woke up the next morning, I snuck out of my room and tiptoed around the house, trying to find something to eat. Candy, food, chips, pop, anything. I looked in the trash and found something they ate for dinner that night. I couldn't open the ice box because she would hear me. My mom would passed out with a wine bottle beside her. Thunderbird was her drink. Hurrying back to my room, I shut my door softly and ran over to a corner and started eating the bread and meat so fast because I knew if I got caught, it was over. My mom was good at not feeding me or sending me to bed without something to eat. I was so hungry that I would look out my dirt window like a lost dog, thinking to myself how can I escape this room and eat my next meal. Just then I heard, "Adam, come here."

I turned around and looked at the door thinking to myself, did she see me? Did I leave a clue or what have I done? I opened the door walked out in my dirty tee shirt with no shoes, socks or pants with pee and shit stains in them. As I walked down the hall I heard my mom cough. I stood there looking at my mom while she was sitting there on the couch swaying back and forth with her brown eyes and short hair. She looked up at me and said, "If you find my cigarettes I'll give you a sandwich."

A smile came over my face because I knew that wouldn't be hard because she smoked a lot and there is always a pack laying some-where. But when you're looking for her cigs and she'd been drinking there's two things you need to know: number one, she's talking about her new pack and two, you'd better hurry up and find them. So I started looking in the chair and around the tables. The house wasn't in too bad of shape because my mom cleaned up all the time. I knew where they were but I was so glad to be out of that room that I took my time. I hated that smelly room and I didn't want to go back in it. Every time she'd shut that door I'd go crazy, yelling, kicking walls, kicking the door and then she'd open the door and say, "Shut the fuck up and go to bed."

After thinking about that stuff I look up and realized that I was in the kitchen looking for something to eat. I quickly looked around for food, drink, a piece of bread or something before she called me but found nothing. I couldn't open the icebox for she would hear it. Our icebox was old and brown and when you opened it, it made this loud sound that would hurt your ears. The light would flicker off and on so at nighttime if Mom turned the lights off in the kitchen, you had to grab something out the icebox quick before the light went off. "Adam, my damn cigarettes ain't the fuck in there. Get in here."

As I ran slowly out the kitchen weighing thirty-nine pounds and with a height of three feet or less, I would enter the room, and she would look up at me and say, "What are you doing?"

I would say, "Nothing," then start looking around some more. I knew where they were, but I was too afraid to go over by her, thinking that as soon as I bent down to pick them up from under the couch, she would hit me in the head. And that usually hurt because my hair was thin and very curly. I crawled over by her and lay down to grab the cigarettes from beside her feet under the couch. I found them. Now can I have some food, pop, cookies anything, I thought. I yelled, I found them. She slowly pulled out a cigarette and picked up the lighter and looked at me as she lit her cigarette and blew the smoke out. "Thanks," she said. "What you want to eat?"

I smiled at her while my mind was going crazy, thinking about what to ask for, trying to say what I wanted, but the words wouldn't come out. No matter what food popped in my head, I just couldn't open my mouth because I was too happy and smiling. Then I heard my mom say to me, "You want some chicken?"

I just nodded yes but really meaning no. It was Saturday, no school, and I wanted a bowl of cereal like my brother would be getting. I wanted to watch TV, but I knew that if I said no that meant I'd get nothing, so I didn't make her mad.

Now, whenever this happened, she would have me sit down by her feet and talk to me. She would say, "I don't know why your dad ain't here with his dumbass."

But who wanted to be around that shit everyday. She would talk about the white man and how when he'd come over to get his rent, he would be mad because he ain't getting nothing for this rat house. Then she would just start crying. I would look up at her, thinking, why did she do the things she did to people? To me? We didn't do anything to her; I knew my mom could be nice, but she was also mean. But I was feeling sad for her and I didn't know why. Only thing I knew was that I was eating chicken and I'm not in that cage of a bedroom.

As time went on, I learned to accept how I was living and that she was my mom. I didn't have a good role model, so it was either my mom or her boyfriend, and that was hard because my mom beat me, and her boyfriend was beating me and he was a drinker. I used to hear my mom say about men that if you buy them shoes, they'd walk out of your life, and if you feed them good they won't never leave. And she would say, "Adam, I'm going to show you how to make it in this world."

As I was growing up, times were changing, and so was my mom. I remember when I was six, that was when I started really understanding my mom. Now my mom kept me by her side ever since I was walking. She told me what to do as I spent time looking for my sisters and my brother's stuff, helped my mom with washing clothes, going to the store, or cleaning the house. While my sisters and brother would tear the house up, watch TV, or eat up everything they wanted to or just run around things, I wasn't allowed to do anything. No, I had to pull a basket of wet clothes outside for my mom to hang up, and it was heavy. We had one of those washers that had a ringer where you plugged it in and pulled this knob out, while the wheel inside would turn back and forth. On top there was a ringer and two rollers tightly put together. When you turned the handle, it would start rolling forward, and it would roll backward too. Our washer was old. My mom washed clothes every day, sometimes all day till she got tired. She would say to me, "That's why I need you to help me because you're strong, and I can't do this by myself."

I would just say, "Yeah." Anything else would get me beat. We would go out, and I would hand my mom the clothes while she hung them, and if I didn't shake them she would say, "Dumbass, shake them." Then she'd push me down hard, but I dared not cry. My mom was strong and proud, took care of home, and provided for her kids, but she was very mean and loved to drink and play cards. I knew I wanted to be like her, strong and knowing what to do when in trouble. She wasn't a tall woman nor was she big in weight, but I knew not to make her mad, or you would get beat. I remember when my oldest sister stayed after school for some reason, and my mom sent me over to one of her school friends' house to see if she was there. She wasn't, and I came back home and told my mom. She told me to go down into the basement and get the hose; that was the one we filled the washer up with. I looked at my mom and said okay and ran to the basement door with a smile on my face. I didn't want to go down there because there was never any light, and it was dirty and smelly. Rats were down there, and trash. And when you flushed the toilet, the poop would come up out this hole. But still just to see somebody else get beat instead of me was worth it.

As I came back, I heard my mom yelling, so I closed the door. As I turned around to walk over to my mom, I couldn't because I saw my big sister crying for the first time. I was shocked. I thought I was the only one who got beat and was scared of my mom. I soon felt scared for her.

Walking slowly toward my mom with my hand halfway out, I handed the hose over, afraid of what she was going to do. My sister got beat for staying after school to try out for track. I learned later by hearing my two older sisters being mad at each other that one wouldn't tell Mom where she was. Well, she got her beatdown, and it was loud. I didn't know what to think; I've never seen my sister get in trouble. I lay in my bed, holding my sheet tight, afraid that if my mom got mad she might come in and start hitting me. Sometimes she would because drinking made her mad, and that particular night she was drinking. I was six years old, My mom and I had a different kind of friendship. I knew she needed me and I needed her. Whenever my mom needed something or wanted something done I was the man, and I was glad. Now everything didn't change, just some things. I still didn't get to eat all of the time, but she stopped beating me when someone came over and told her they had seen me in town begging, when I should have been in school, or that I was in a store stealing. I never understood why I got beat for stealing, especially when I stole for her. At six years of age, my mom taught me a lot, and as I looked back on it, she was really showing me how to take care of family and self. I remember the times when my mom went out and gambled our money away. We were on welfare, and there was six of us plus Mom and her boyfriend in a four-bedroom home with two living rooms, a big kitchen, one bathroom, and a basement. We moved about every other year after my dad left because he found my mom was having sex with his best friend. My sister had their dad who I've never seen. Maybe I was too small to remember at the time, plus I wasn't always around. My mom chose my dad's best friend, and that was who her boyfriend was. All the homes my mom chose were messed up with bad plumbing, cheap rent—just a bad house. We did our best with the homes; the problems came when it was time to pay rent. She would tell the landlord some lie, and they would talk. Then he would leave, and she would shut the door and say, "That's how you do white people that don't like blacks."

I guess I could say I learned a lot from my mom because she made me learn, and she kept me out of school until I got locked up. I used to go to pre-K and kindergarten, but I got kicked out of both. While in pre-K, I used to go to this house by the fairgrounds with a red door, and when I walked up to it, I would be scared. But I opened the door and saw all the people inside with kids laughing and playing. I remember that my mom left me there and said, "I'll be back later to get you." She then turned around and left. I was scared because she'd never left me before, only with my older sister at home. I remember playing, eating, and stealing. I used to go in their pocketbooks, taking their wallet to the bathroom. I would take all of the money out and put it in my shoes. Then I'd wait for my mom to come and tell her I found some money, so she would let me go out-side and play. She'd say nice things to me and treat me like the other kids. "No," she would say. "You didn't find no money, boy." Then she would knock me upside my head. Now I know what you're saying, how could a boy who's five and a half to six years old do these things? My mom was an alcoholic and hung out at bootleg joints, flirting with men, playing cards for money, cursing women out about their man, or showing me how to play cards. Most of the time she was winning and picking the pockets of the hardworking men with good money. She would give it to me to hold. They called her Lady Tunk, and she was good. It would be four men and one woman sitting at the card table, and everybody knew mom and her son Adam. While she'd be winning, she would take me into the bathroom and give me her money and say, "Put this in your shoe, and don't take it off and stay with me. And if anything happens, run home. I'll be there."

She told me "Sit still, don't move or say anything." I went every-where with my mom, to the bank on welfare day, the electric com-pany, the gas company, grocery stores, and shopping for my sisters and brothers. I would go next door to beg for money, sugar, milk, etc., asking for food for me. When I asked people if I could have something to eat, they would say, "Does your mom feed you?" And I would tell them no. Then they would say, "Come on, your mom ain't like that."

They wouldn't believe me, and I would say to myself that no matter what I say about my mom, people see her differently. They believed that my mom was one lady who loved her kids. They just didn't know because I was taught don't tell anybody what goes on in the Johnson family. We all, fifteen kids total, lived with secrets that we're not allowed to speak about for being blinded by the veil of my mom, Georgia. She was the Only woman I've loved. I just didn't know this at the time. I remember my mom not having food in the house, so we would walk uptown to the store, and my mom would ask the owner for credit until she got her check. He would say okay. It might be three days before the check came, two weeks before, maybe even thirty days. You never knew what my mom would do because she always twisted things for her kids no matter what the costs. Nothing was too good for her kids.

Hamburgers, noodles, milk, eggs, bread, sauce, Pepsi, cigarettes, chips, candy bars, suckers, this was the stuff my mom bought when she got credit or borrowed money from someone. She might pay them back or not because she'd say, "I'm Georgia, and ain't no bitch, man, or woman going to beat my ass." And she meant that. At 5'2" and weighing 110 pounds, my mom was dangerous but not with weapons—she could fight. My mom loved to gamble and drink because she looked at it this way: "I have a man who ain't shit, seven kids and no job. I'm forty-five to years old, and I have to take care of my family."

To my mom, gambling meant making more money, and she was down for that. She would play fifty, a hundred, two hundred, a thousand dollars a hand because she was good at what she did. Now remember, whatever my mom did, I did. When she got drunk, that was when my mom would tell me how to do things. She would tell me over and over, don't get caught and don't ever tell. I studied my mom, my brother, my sisters, and my mom's boyfriend. They would have me steal for them, but afterward they would beat and hit me, treating me like trash. I still couldn't sit on the furniture and slept on a nasty mattress for months. I wasn't allowed out of my room once she told me to go in there, or I'd get beat with pipes, extension cords, broom handles, the fat stick, etc. It hurt. It just depended on whether or not she was drunk or just mad. The fat stick was thick, hard, and strong; you would hurt before it broke. What they didn't know was that I knew what they liked and didn't like. I knew how to make my move. My mom showed me how to keep an eye on people, to watch what they would do and how they would act. It was hard to act like you don't see what is going on. For five years my mom trained me on how to get money for her and the family. I knew my sisters went to school and liked to go to games in town or visit over their friends' houses. Back then, my mom didn't trust nobody, so either my sisters went together, or I had to go with them. Yes. They would ask me to steal candy and other things and then tell on me. I would get sent to that dark room, get my behind beat. Yes, I loved it when we went to football games. Once my sisters looked away, I would wander off to steal and eat. I knew that when they found me, Lisa was going to hit me in the head all the way home, saying, "That's why I don't take you niggers anywhere with me because you are dumb."

I really didn't care if they kept me in that room, for I knew I had money, candy, and cigarettes. My mom would be mad at me and beat the shit out of me. Then later after they went to bed, she would open the door and tell me to come out. I would wipe my tears away, adjust my eyes to the light, and walk into the TV room. As I sat on the floor, she would say, "You know you shouldn't be stealing. What if you get caught? Who's going to help me around here and watch over the family?"

I would just say, "I don't know."

I sat there thinking to myself, *You have sent me to stores with no money, no nothing but a list of stuff to come back with*. And when I would ask where the money was, she would look at me with that black coffee skin, mean look in her eyes, and reply, "You don't need money, and don't forget my cigarettes and pop." My mom loved cigs and Pepsi more than anything. I was shocked because the first time I did it, I begged everybody in town for the money to get items on the list. I told the people I had to get these items, or my mom would beat me. The white people would help, but the black people would point and say things to themselves. But I really was telling the truth; I would get the shit beat out of me if I came back home empty-handed. Now when it came to the cigs, I gave the note to the store owner or some black person who knew my mom, and they would get it for me and ask, "Where is your mom? And tell her don't be sending you out here."

I would make up a story like she's sick or that my brother was hurt or something. I got so good when my mom was broke, I would tell her, "I know where some money is." She would ask me where and I would tell her, "Let me go out, and I'll get it." I'd gotten so good at my game that my mom couldn't keep up with me. She'd taught me well. Sometimes I would already have money hidden in my room or hidden outside. I made sure whenever I went anywhere to hide what I stole. When she said okay, I would leave and go play football with my cousin and friends. I didn't get to play with them much, and they would ask where I'd been or how come I didn't come to school that much. I would make up a lie like I was sick or that something happened at home. Then I would treat all of them with something from the store. I would pull all this money out to impress them, and it worked. They would say, "Man, where you get that?"

"My mom," I would reply, or "I work for my mom's boyfriend."

They would ask me for money, so I started giving them some. I would go back home late after dark and act like I'd been trying to get more money to bring home. Sometimes it worked, then other times she would come and look for me or send my sisters after me. But she never knew I was stealing candy every day for my sisters, Snickers, Reese's Peanut Butter Cups, M&Ms, whatever, and they didn't care. At first they didn't want me around them because they would say, "No telling who's after you or what you've done."

I was only six going on seven, but they got me stealing for them. I had food, candy, pop, cigarettes, and money hidden in my room. So when she didn't feed me, I had stuff but nobody could know because they would take it, and I'd get beat. While everyone else slept, I would eat all night, open the window, and throw my trash out. They wouldn't know it was mine because I was the only one who cleaned up outside. Sometimes when I didn't get enough to eat or wanted more candy, I would do stuff to get sent to my room. I'd get up and walk around, pick up a toy, walk into the kitchen, or hit Troy. That would get me a first-class kick in the middle of my back and a hit with the belt. And Troy always had that belt because he loved hitting me with it like he'd seen Mom do it. It was worth it because I wouldn't have to get beat all day.

If Mom drank early in the day, she would think about bad time, hurt, feeling that it would make her turn mad. Then there were times I would be sleepy but not allowed to lay down and take a nap. When I did, my mom, Troy, Tammi, or Lisa would kick me anywhere on my body real hard and say, "Wake up! You know you're not allowed to sleep out here."

I've had my eyes busted, bleeding, my mouth busted, and cuts open all over my body. My leg was broken, and my arms have hurt for weeks. I've even had a high-heeled shoe stuck in my head. Put it inside my head, when she hit me with the heel. All this happened over and over for four years back to back, with me saying nothing to no one outside of the home. My mom took me to the doctor for my leg once after she kicked me down the steps when I was five. I couldn't walk for days, and she would hit me if I took too long to do something for her. Even though my leg was hurting badly, I had to get up every time she wanted something. I used to soft cry a lot, which means a lot of quiet crying with no sound. She would say, "Nothing wrong with you, and ain't nobody going to feel for no pissy shitty boy like you." My mom started using me a lot for errands and store running. I started taking longer to come home because I had moved up in my skills. With no birthday presents, no Christmas presents or Easter, I made my own because my mom said to me, "If you can steal from stores, people's homes, and pick pockets right in front of me, why would I give these things to you?"

I was stealing really well from family, friends, breaking into homes just looking for money or food. Remember, there were seven of us, and somebody didn't get a lot to eat...and that was me. My mom didn't come into my room too much because It smelled like piss and shit because that was where they kept me most of my growing up. During the winter, my heat register didn't work, so I could pee there until she smelled it. I couldn't open the windows because Mom locked, no she nailed my windows shut, so I couldn't open them. I used to poop out my window in cups, bags, clothes, or whatever when I had to go really bad. Mom would not let me come out, no matter how much I called her name or told her that I really needed to go. She would say, "I'm going to beat your ass if you keep it up." Or sometimes she would find it in my clothes or out the window, and she'd beat me bad, really bad. Then sometimes she would let me go. I was scared of my mom.

Sometimes we just didn't have enough food. I was really mad every holiday because Mom bought me something (rare?), but Troy would take it and then break it. Troy got a lot of things, but I was not allowed to touch anything, or I would get hit. By now you're probably wondering if I'm telling you the truth. Well, I want you to know that if you are doing or have been doing any of this to a child, another human being, an elderly person or anyone, stop. You have fucked up their lives, but there is a chance that they might make it back. Now I'm going to tell you some things for all of you who don't believe in yourself. Don't stop keep pushing on because people say you won't, but you shall. My mom started getting visits from school officials concerned about why I was not attending school. She was running out of lies, and they wanted me in school, or she would be in trouble. She would have me hide while she told them that I was sick in bed, out of town, or with my dad. Anyway, I knew, and she knew that once I was in school that meant she would have to treat me just like the rest of my siblings. She had to buy me clothes, shoes, wash me up, and give me a new bed, and no more eating on the floor. I was seven years old at the time, but I had been out of school since I was five. That meeting was a good and bad day for me because I knew she had to do it, and she hated it because she made me do everything. After they left, she turned around and snapped, "You think you're smart, you and those white folks. You just want them to take you away don't you?"

I got beaten up for that, but the school officials won, and I was enrolled into the second grade. I couldn't read, didn't know my letters, numbers, or how to spell my name. This went on for about a week before my teachers started calling and sending notes home. Troy told lies on me. Teachers brought me home, saying, "Adam's not learning, and your son ate all of the kids' packed lunches. He steals and hits the other kids."

My mom's only response to this white man was this, "I told you dumb people he can't be in school." But he replied that I'd better be there. She said, "Don't you come tellin' me what to do. Y'all wanted him now, deal with it. He's there, not here." Sitting there listening, to that they were saying about me, saying these things like I'm not there. Man I couldn't believe it. I was winning; she couldn't keep me home no more. I would walk to school with my sister before me and Troy; we were in the same building. Tammi was in the fourth grade, I was in the second grade, and Troy was in kindergarten or at home. I was happy that I was free, free from Mom, that room, and the beatings. Soon I started skipping school, breaking into homes, stealing jewelry, bikes, food, and money. I stole shirts and socks from stores by stuffing them around my waist in my coat lining. I'd give them to my mom, sisters, and my brother. I'd give my sisters and brother candy bars just so they would love me or at least like me. Every time my mom asked me where I got this or that, I would say I found it. She would take it, hit me, and then send me to bed. What could she really say to me when she was the one who told me to steal, ask, and beg for the things that we needed? I was seven. Yes. My mom accepted the fact that she couldn't keep me home anymore without getting in trouble with the white people. So much happened every year. I just want you to know that time took a long time to come.

We lived in a town with mostly white and poor black people that I knew. They really didn't like black people unless you cleaned or worked for them. They wouldn't even look at you, and they would say that the character of Superman came from their will. I learned so much from when I got beat, how I watched others, being locked in that room, etc. I remembered what my grandma said to me, "Someday, you will be somebody, and just because you don't have something don't mean you can't take care of what you do have. I know your mom treat you bad, but she cares about you, and you know how she can be sometimes."

I put all that to use. I started meeting people like teachers, who worked with me after school. They stopped telling on me when I got into trouble, and my mom didn't like this. One of my teachers was nice, and she started showing me to other people. Remember when I told you that I thought things were going to change when I went to school? Well, they didn't. I was still wearing Troy's clothes and shoes. I still slept on a pissy mattress and got whooped. She started keeping me home from school after I had gotten used to eating lunch, play-ing, laughing, or stealing from others on the way home. I continued to sneak out the house when she got drunk. I was finally learning about the outside. I knew my sisters' friends, our cousins, people around us, and school kids. One morning I woke up ready to go to school. My mom let me get ready, after I had looked for everyone else's stuff as usual. I sat and waited in the living room on the floor while Troy and Tammi got ready for school. They would be watching TV, putting on their clothes, moving slowly, and asking Mom for help. Now I had already looked for their shoes, pants, and shirts and dressed myself, but I was not allowed to watch TV. As my mom said, "Let's go," I got up and started walking to the door. My mom said, "I need you to stay home today." I said, "Okay," took my coat off, and felt good but scared too. I knew that I had to build up enough confidence to ask Mom for food, to watch TV, or to go outside and play. Sometimes she said yes and sometimes no. Today she said yes, but she turned the TV on for me. I went to the grocery store with her, and we had a good time because if she didn't drink, we would get something to eat or talk. She would tell me what stuff is or how to get things done. Mom always talked with me and to me. Yes. I never knew my dad. When I was five years old my mom, Olivia, Troy, Lorri, Lisa, and Tammi went for a ride. We pulled up at this bar, and my mom got out, walked up to this brown door and went in. We were left outside in the car. It was hot that day, and the next thing I knew my mom came out with this man, and they were mad at each other, yelling, talking loudly. My mom walked over to the car, got in, and drove off. She was crying. I looked at her from the back seat thinking to myself, what happened? Did somebody hit her? I smiled at first, then I was sad, thinking about what might have happened or who made her cry. My mom then said that we were going to the dairy for ice cream. There used to be a Dairy Queen on this country back road, but we didn't go; instead she took us home. Now this was when everything started happening. I hated my stepdad because he has sex with my dad's wife. Me at six years old, my mom used to give me notes and some money and sent me to the store to get stuff, and I had better not come back without it. I couldn't add or subtract so my mom would show me five-, ten-, twenty-, fifty-, and hundred-dollar bills. So say I'm buying a pack of cigs out of five dollars, Mom would say, "You'll get three one-dollar bills and some coins."

She then showed me the difference between quarters, dimes, and nickels. This was when I learned how to count money and what to steal. When I was in school, I used to bully people. I would tell them if they didn't bring me money that I would beat them up. And

I even told them what kind of money to bring. I was bad. I'd ask to go to the bathroom and then go through my teacher's pocketbook before going back to class. I stole stuff that my mom said was valuable, like money and jewelry. I knew that this made her happy. I stole just because my mom would be nice to me or give me something to eat. Now there were times that I stole something when she never told me to get it, and I was caught. She would beat the shit out of me right then and there. I didn't understand why she'd beat me and starve me for stealing when she had taught me what to do. After my mom found out about me stealing for myself and for kids that bullied me, she started keeping me in. She only let me out when she needed something from the store, or when she sent me to look for her boyfriend. I was six years old, and I was smart. No, just street and mouth. I knew how to steal, lie, and write notes like my mom letter for letter. She taught me small words and how they made sentences. Yes, I would write notes like my mom for candy, pop, cigs, so I wouldn't get caught and take the cigs home to make her happy. My mom was hearing around town how Georgia got a bad kid, and this was making her mad. "Did you hear he stole this?" "He broke into that." "The police picked him up, and he is only five or six years old." We lived in a small town with about seven thousand people, and everybody knew everybody. I know some things I say in this book might come back to haunt me, but let me say this: I paid my sins to God and the police. Kids that I knew used to let me come over to play, and I would steal from their moms and take things from their home just to give to my mom. But nothing changed. Things were still the same with me; I got beat and still had to clean the house, etc. I was often late to school because I was too busy looking to break into somebody's home or go to a store to walk around. I would tell them that my mom sent me for milk or something. After school, I would go over somebody's house to play. I had some great friends, some of the best friends that I ever knew. There was this beautiful girl named Lisa who I was in love with but knew I was not allowed to be with. I walked her home one day when I was about seven years old. It was a nice day outside, and the bell had just rung, and I was going to ask her if I could carry her books. I knew that my sisters were coming to get me from class, and I was in trouble with my teacher for eating all of the other kids' lunches. I took their money from them, and the ones who weren't giving me their money, I would just steal their money out of their desk or pockets. Or I stole the lunch count because back then parents sent in money for lunch. The teacher's desk, middle drawer, in a small brown envelope. Six to eight dollars, maybe more, if there was a field trip. I looked up at Lisa as she sat there with her long brown and golden hair tightly braided in two ponytails hanging down her back. She always had a smile and always had on the best of clothes and shoes. She always said hi to people. There was something about her that just made me want her to be my girlfriend. It was hard for me to talk to her because, at recess, all the kids wanted to play with her, and at lunch they all sat by her. I had to sit in the office for lunch; the teachers didn't trust me. And when the bell rang for school to be out, Lisa was the first one out the door because she was a walker. I couldn't catch her because my teacher stuck me in the back of the class, at the end near the corner of the room. If you're wondering why I sat in the back, well, one reason was due to me bullying kids. And if I acted up in class, she would march right over to me and yank my desk around to where my back was against the class. She would always say, "And don't you show your face until I say."

I couldn't stand my teacher. But today I had a plan. Five minutes before the bell rang, I asked my teacher if I could go to the bathroom. She said, "The bell is about to ring. Can it wait?"

"No," I replied. "I have to do the number two, and I can't hold it." The whole class laughed and so did Lisa. As I looked at her, she looked back at me. And just for one minute I looked at her, and she looked at me, and I smiled too. The teacher said, "Okay, but when you're done come back. I have a note for your mom."

"Okay," I replied as I smiled at Lisa and walked out. I shut the door, walked four steps, and turned around. I was leaning against the wall to wait for Lisa. I knew that my sisters would be coming to get me, but I wanted to walk Lisa home and leave that bad note at school. I was going to get in trouble, but I didn't care. I was going to ask Lisa if I could walk her home.

"Adam. *Adam*," said the principal. I couldn't hear her calling my name because I was daydreaming about walking Lisa home. She called my name again.

"Oh, hi Principal Skinner"

"What did you do this time, Adam, to be out here?" she said.

Scared, she would take me back in class, which meant no walking home with Lisa, as well as listening to my sisters' taunts about how Mom would react to my note, I just shrugged my shoulders. "Oh, I was just laughing in class."

"Now you be good and stop that," she replied as she walked by with her horn in her hand, headed toward the big kids.

I was happy. No sisters yet and then *ding, ding*. The door opens, and out walks Lisa. I stepped up and asked, "Lisa, how you doing?"

"Fine."

"Can I walk with you?"

She said yes.

I was so happy as we walked out of school like we were boyfriend and girlfriend. I didn't want this to end. As we talked and walked, I made her laugh, and she told me she had a little brother and her mom and dad and that they were Indians. I told her I was an Indian too but when she asked me what kind, I told her I didn't know. Then she didn't say nothing. Now that I think about it, that made me look bad, not knowing what I was or where I came from. We walked toward this beautiful house where I wished my family could live. We went down this hill where I could see trees, the woods, and there were two houses on each side of the road. When the road ended, Lisa said, "This is my house." I looked at it, and it seemed like a nice home with pretty paint and flowers. Her mom opened the door. She was a pretty lady with long black hair and brown golden skin. Lisa said, "This is Adam, and he's in my class. He asked me if he could walk with me."

Wow, I never heard anyone say something that nice to me or about me. Her mom said hello, and I think I said hi. She said, "Don't be too long, your dad will be home soon."

Lisa and I talked a little while longer, then we said bye. I started walking up the hill, smiling to myself, being very happy. Then I heard, "Adam." I turned around, and there was Lisa in the middle of the road, and she said, "Will you be in class tomorrow?"

I said yes.

She smiled and said, "I'll see you then."

I turned around and started running really, really fast up the hill. I was happy because the prettiest girl in my class let me walk her home, said good things about me to her mom, and asked if I would be in class the next day. Wow! I knew I was in trouble, but I didn't care because I had just walked Lisa home. I remembered the good things because they rarely happened, but the bad was always with me. I got home with a bag for my mom, a pack of Pall Mall cigarettes and a can of pop. When I walked in, the sheriff was there, and I knew who he was because he used to come to our home on Fridays for my mom and her boyfriend. Plus, he lived down the street from us, and his son and I were friends. My mom looked at me, and I handed her the bag and walked away. As they talked some more, my sisters asked where I had been. I told them I had walked this girl home. Tammi laughed at me and said, "You don't have any friends. Don't nobody like you." Tammi was a year older than me. Lisa said, "You're a liar, and that's why you're going to get a whoopin'."

Lorri said, "Just tell the truth, somebody just broke into a house and stole some things, and they think you did it."

"I didn't," I cried. "I was somewhere else."

My mom came in and said, "Adam what did you do?"

"Nothing."

"You're lying. Why else would he come over here and say something to me about this? If we have to move because of you, I'm going to beat you."

Mr. Brown was a sheriff, and he knew what was going on in his town, and he knew that I stole because his best friend caught me stealing out of his store. A seventeen-year-old boy named Billy who lived next to me said I'd pay for it. He is my neighbor's little brother. That's how I come to Jesus. I went to church with this guy by the name of Billy, who lived next door to us. Billy and my sisters, Lorri and Lisa, went to school together. I had some friends named, the Petersons, the Kellys, and Tom, who had a twin sister. We ended up moving because people were talking about us for the things I was doing in church. I used to eat the cookies and drink the juice. I stole the church money out of Sunday school and went into people's pocketbooks and coats. I gave all of the money to my mom, so I would be able to go outside and play. I never went back to that school, and I never got a chance to see Lisa again. I remember we moved to this house far away and the only thing around us was this bar across the street and some houses here and there. The reason my mom moved so far was that she got tired of people talking about things her son was doing. My sisters hated me and didn't want to be seen with me. Sometimes they would walk to school without me, so my mom told me, "You can't do nothing."

There were no stores, and all the people stayed at home. But I knew something that my mom didn't know—I was sneaking out my window, going to the bar and eating. She loved to drink, and there was a bar across the street, so that meant she would need to go get cigs or take a note over to them. My mom didn't work, but she was on welfare, and her boyfriend worked. But sometimes the money ran out, and there were times when she needed things. The bar became her home, and the people who owned it were glad because my mom kept a bill with them. My mom would tell people that I would work for them in order to help out around the house. So I learned how to work for them to get things to eat by saying that my mom had sent me over. I started sneaking out of the windows in my room. I was doing this for quite some time, but I didn't know that my mom was smarter than me. She nailed my windows shut and made me sleep with her in the living room. While she'd be on the couch covered up, I would sleep on the floor in the corner with no cover. I would sneak up at night and steal something to eat or look for things to cover me up with like shirts, pants, towels, or whatever was lying around. No, my mom told me that I slept in the living room in order to protect her if somebody broke in. My mom never slept in a bedroom; she always slept in the front room to make sure my older sisters never snuck out. I was her man, and she needed me. Somewhere down the line my mom started feeling down about something because she played "Leaving on a Midnight Train to Georgia." She loved Gladys Knight, and I still listen to her today.

I was into everything now. Stealing, lying, carrying guns, robbing, bullying people, shakedowns. I played a little bit; I lived on a farm, so I could throw rocks, play in the woods and creeks. One time me and some friends were going swimming, and I didn't know how, so they were going to teach me. They jumped in, played around, and then told me to jump in. I don't know why I listened to them because when we played together, I was the one who always got hurt. I don't know who pushed me, but I was pushed and the next thing I knew I was in the water. I tried to get out, but I couldn't. I thought they would save me, but they were laughing at me. When I started to drown, someone pulled me out. There were about four of us, and I was the smallest out of the four and the only one who was black. As I continued to cough and gag up water, they took off running. I guess they were going home. The next time I saw them they laughed and said, "Hey, didn't we drown you?"

They still came over to see if I was allowed out, and I would go even though I knew they were up to something. But it was better than being home and having to look for something or someone. And I didn't have to watch my mom sing drunk to me, while blaming me for various things that had happened. I wondered if she was really blaming me or my dad because my mom would tell me that he was a good dad but didn't know shit about a woman.

The boys I hung out with taught me how to shoot cows with BB guns, how to break into houses when people left, and how to fight. Being the only black boy in that town meant I would get beat up on, or they would come get me if I bothered them. If they didn't like your family, they would call you names, throw stuff at you like rocks, call you nigger. I always got beat up by them white boys from the farm side, but on some days we just played bombs away. Anything goes…There were these dirt hills about twenty to thirty feet in the air, and we would climb them and act like we were kings of them and knock each other off by throwing rocks at each other. Whoever got hit the hardest would fall off. Well, on this particular day we played, I was going to get them back one by one. We were having fun running up and down the hills with rocks and sticks poking out from them. Then we started throwing rocks, and this was my chance, so I picked up this big rock and threw it at one of the boys real hard in the face. I don't know what happened after that because I started running before I threw the rock, and when I looked back, all of them were coming after me. I lived far, so I ran all the way home while they were yelling at me, black names, bad names. I was out of breath when I got home. My mom asked me why I was not out playing. I told her I got tired of those white boys beating me up, so I hit one with a rock. Mom replied, "You know they're going to kick your ass in school." While my mom was drinking, it didn't matter what you said, as long as you said the word white before saying anything else. She didn't like white people at all. The rent man never got his money, and the only reason she paid her light bill and gas was to play her records and drink. We were at home when I heard a knock at the door. Evening of the same day, my mom got up drunk, falling here and there. I tried to catch her so she didn't fall...I got my ass kicked a lot for not helping her. As we walked into the kitchen, my mom yelled, "Who the hell is this?" Opening the door, this big white man was standing there. I said to myself, the rent man done sent somebody over to get his money. Not true, for this man said to my mom, "Your nigga boy hit my boy in the head with a rock."

She looked at me and hit me with the flying back hand then turned to him and said, "Get the fuck off my porch!" and slammed the door. From that point on I really loved my mom. Any other time she would have pulled my pants off and beat my legs, foot, and butt, but she didn't. She let it slide.

In school I would talk stuff to them white boys; I threw stuff at them and then ran. Sometimes I would just walk up to any boy and hit him in the face. I started to like fighting. I saw my mom hit men with frying pans, knives, whatever, so I started doing it to kids and asking for their money. I scared them so bad that their moms and dads got together and told my mom she'd have to move out of their town. This happened a few times. Now the last time we moved, I had told my mom that I found some money buried in the dirt where we played. She was happy, so I must have stolen a lot. She took me into the house, gave me some, and told me not to tell nobody. She didn't know where it came from, but she knew it didn't come from the dirt. I remember being in school, and my mom came and picked us up. Back then everybody was under one school, elementary and high school combined. School was out at three for big kids and three thirty for little kids. We were walking fast, mom cussing, yelling at us to keep up. We've never had a new car, but we had a station wagon. When we got in, my sisters were mad about something. My mom said, "We're packing and going to see Grandma." I was smiling because that meant she would be nice to me and feed me. My grandma knew my mom was drunk and abusive. We had to move over to my grandma's house, and I knew my mom couldn't be mean to me over there because my grandma loved me.

Grandma was cool. She would talk to us about everything, showing us how to clean, working in her shop, giving away clothes. Now I don't know why we left, but my mom was really mad, and she left a lot of our stuff behind. My older sisters were crying about their things, but I wasn't. I didn't have anything. I didn't have toys, clothes, a bed, sheets, shoes—nothing. It was just me. I was in a town where no one knew me, and I didn't know them. Only thing I knew was when we visited Grandma it was family reunion time.

Before I started school late because my mom would say, "You don't need to go for you're not going to listen to them. You're always stealing or fighting, so you'll go tomorrow." But by the time my mom would remember to send me back, children's services would drop by. My mom didn't like anybody telling her what to do, so there were times that she would keep me home. I always found some reason to get out the house. My mom didn't care because she would send me places after dark, during the winter, out for my family at all times. I stole for them, I hurt people for them. I guess everything started happening when we moved to Ohio.

I knew my cousins in that town and everybody knew my mom. Mom started taking me to juke joints, stores, banks, and around people that she knew. Mom called me her right-hand man. At that time I was seven years old, and I started breaking into homes and stealing mail. That's how I got my mom to let me out of the house. People would put money in their mailboxes to pay bills. When I first found out about the money, I opened somebody's mail and took the money home to my mom. That would get me dinner for the night, and she would buy food, beer, wine, and cigs. The family would be nice to me, but I still slept on a pee-pee mattress in dirty clothes. My mom loved my sisters and brother. She bought them everything, did everything for them, but for me no. Mom would say, "You can steal, why worry about you?" My sisters thought it was cool to go with my mom wherever she went, but it wasn't. People would say, hey are you going to pay me, she would say no. But we can play for what I owe you. Mom would tell people about me sneaking out of the house, stealing, all of the stuff that she actually taught me to do. But she acted like it was my idea. I've never said this to anyone, but I wanted to kill my mom and family. They were mean to me, beat me all the time, and didn't buy me nothing. They fed me when they wanted to. I used to lie on the floor, wishing the house would burn down, or that the police would come and take her away. I thought a lot about what if. I had an aunt in Cleveland, and they would come down twice a year to visit my grandma. Mom didn't like her sister at all, but my Aunt would always ask, "Where's Adam?" I loved seeing her because she was nice; she dressed real good and had a nice car. My Uncle was nice too; he didn't talk much, and my aunt said he worked a lot. Aunt would ask, "You want to leave with me?" I would answer yes, but my mom would say, "Not him, so quit asking." But every time they came down, Aunt would say, "You're coming with me." Mom and Aunt argued a lot over me because whenever they came, something was always wrong with me, cuts here, black-and-blue marks, or a black eye. My mom loved to beat me when she drank and would tell me not to run from her. I was so scared that I just stood there and let her beat on me. Then I learned to stop crying, and she really got mad then. That's when she came with a new idea to lock me in my room, sliding my food under the door in the dark. I was scared of the rats and roaches in my room. My mom would just say, "You're a man now. You'll be okay." There were times when I would hit a rat over my food. They would play in my room. I could hear them running, talking, coming onto my bed. I couldn't yell or nothing because my mom would throw something at the door and say, "Don't make me come in there." I would spend all my time in this room, so I would stuff clothes in holes under doors. Keep the cold out. My room was cold and smelly from not being allowed to go to the bathroom. Mom would get mad at me because I punched holes in my bedroom walls. I used to act like they were my mom and family and beat on them. I hated them and that's all I thought about. I was too scared of Mom to tell on her, but I wanted to. Teachers would ask, "What happened Adam?" when they saw the scars. I would just reply that I got jumped. One day my teacher said something to me about being hurt, and she wanted to speak with my mom. My teacher would ask if everything was okay at home, and Mom would say like always, "You know how boys are."

I would sit there hoping the teacher would stop talking because I knew I was already in trouble. When we got home, I got my ass beat because the teacher wanted to talk to my mom and that's a no-no. So as always I got in trouble with mom. Mom and I stop acting up with that teacher. So whenever Mom sent me somewhere, it took me hours to come back. I would steal my favorite foods like PayDays, Reese's Peanut Butter Cups, I loved them. I knew that when I went home I would be locked back in my dark, dirty, stinky room with the rats. I remember when my mom bought some rabbits because her boyfriend said he would raise them to sell and eat. Bullshit! They pissed shit and climbed all over me and my bed. I hated those damn rabbits so I killed them. I fed them stuff Mom left for the rats. Yeah I got in trouble about it, but who gives a damn? They were all in my room, and the only time Mom gave me a bath was when I had to go to school with her, and that was it. Mom didn't give a damn about me. My sisters' rooms were clean, nice beds, no locks on doors, and lights in their room. I was only allowed to walk by, but not to go in. My sister Lisa Tammy would say, "Get your dirty ass away from me," and slammed the door. Lorri loved to tell on me, so she could watch me get in trouble. Tammy would come out and say, "You shouldn't be so bad." I think Tammy didn't like Mom beating me at all the time, but she'd better not say nothing.

I knew when I go somewhere with my sister. It was easy for me to make some quick money. I would get up and leave for school, stop at a nice house, and take their mail. I'd walk to school, open it up, and take out the money. Sometimes I stopped by the candy store first and would show my sisters the money at school. "Where you get that?" they'd ask.

"Found it. You want some?"

So they would snatch it and say, "Don't tell Mom." Yeah, like I'm really going to tell on me. The routine was getting old now, and people were in their home watching me closely. If I would walk in their neighborhood, they knew I wasn't allowed or lived there. "Hey, little boy, are you lost? Who are you looking for?" I ignored their questions and just kept walking, looking for mail to give to my mom, so I could go outside and play.

I knew this guy by the name of Nip. I would go by his gas station and steal candy and pop. One day he caught me in the act. Nip was white, about five eleven with blond hair, and he drove a Corvette. Blue. He always had pretty girls coming to see him. His dad owned the biggest car lot in town, and their house was on a hill. Nipp had a younger brother, but I only saw him when he would come inside sometimes. Well, one day mom said, "Adam, go get me some smokes and Pepsi, and you can go outside." I went by Nipp's gas station and asked him if I could make some money, so I could get this stuff for my mom. I started coming by every day after school to see Nipp. He would have me spray water to get the dirt up, sweep, whatever. We became real good friends. I didn't have to beg or steal for Mom no more; Nipp had cigs and Pepsi. When we talked, I told Nipp everything about me. His dad let me come over to his car lot on Saturdays at 7:00 am to clean his cars. It was one dollar for every car. I was up to five cars when Nipp's dad started paying me five dollars a car. I was good at what I did because Mom always had me cleaning. They liked me and let me drink pop with them. I listened to all kinds of white music like "Walk This Way" by AC/DC, nothing black. Sometimes when I was hanging out with Nipp, I felt like I was white and his brother. I never showed my mom where I worked or who I worked for. Mom just would have said to him, "Don't nobody make an ass out of him but me." Now Mom used to get people to think that she didn't know I was doing these things, like my teachers, store owners, neighbors, and family so they took me to see a doctor. I had to talk to him twice a week, every Monday and Friday after school. My mom took me and explained that she had other kids to take care of and wouldn't be staying. He told her that she didn't have to come with me anymore. His office was next door to the courthouse, and as I came in one day, he asked me to have a seat while he finished writing something down. "Okay, Adam," he began, "would you like some milk and cookies?" I told him yes.

I've experienced so much pain that I have to get myself together before I continue this next phase of my story.

The cookies were always different, and he acted like he had made them. I knew that he didn't.

He went from giving me milk to drink to this red Kool-Aid that tasted like sour water. But I didn't say nothing, I was happy to sit in his office after school eating cookies. I could have been at home with Mom getting yelled at and hit. It was around wintertime when my visits with the doctor started getting really good. The doctor said that we could talk about my mom, and she nor anyone else would ever know. Only he and I would know about what was discussed. He asked me how I got that cut above my eye, but I just looked up at him, too scared to say anything about Mom. I knew better. *But maybe he's my friend,* I thought. *He gave me cookies. Lets me look out the windows to watch the snow fall. I even played with his son's trucks and cars.*

So I told him that Mom had hit me. He asked, "Why?"

"Because I couldn't find her cigarettes."

"Where were you at?"

"Home."

"Was anyone else there?"

"Yes, my sisters and little brother."

"Why didn't they help you?"

"They don't like me."

"What do you mean they don't like you?"

"They don't play with me, talk to me, or give me anything. They don't sit with me, nothing. They don't like me because they say it every day and all day."

"Where is your dad at?" he asked.

"I don't know."

"Can you remember the last time you saw him?"

I looked at the doc like, "Why should I tell you?" with a plain look on my face. He said in a soft voice, "I'm only trying to help you." With a smile on his face. I went on to explain that I was about five years old when my mom drove us to this bar, and my mom said she had to get some money to take us to the park. We were laughing and joking in the station wagon. Well, they were cracking on me, and I was crying while they laughed and called me pissy, shitty, and bad luck. "You shouldn't be here. You're ugly with a dirty face and a smell that can't nobody stand. That's why don't nobody sit by you." That was yours truly, Lisa. That's how she joked about you or anyone else. Next thing I knew, my mom came out, saying in a loud voice, "No, Adam, no, no." Then everybody started looking out the front window and hanging out windows, yelling.

"Were you all hanging out the windows of the car?" I said "yes."

I'm in the back of the wagon, I can't see or get out. My sisters were yelling, "Mom, Mom!" They started to cry. I was standing on the seat, trying to see my mom, saying to myself, "Can't nobody help her but me. Just let me out." But I knew if I said anything that my sister would hit me. So I just kept on looking. Then out of nowhere I saw Mom. I was happy, not really knowing why, but a smile was on my face. Mom got in and said, "He's crazy. your dad thinks me and Melvin are fucking." I didn't know what that meant; I just knew Mom said it when something went wrong.

"Did your dad ever come home after that?" the doctor asked.

With my head down I said, "No. Nothing." No one said anything. I was crying. The doctor said, "Okay, Adam, I'll see you tomorrow." He gave me a napkin, patted me on my head, and said, "It's going to be all right." I wiped my eyes and followed him to the door. I quickly asked if I could have another cookie, and he stopped and looked at me. Smiling, he said, "Go ahead." I really liked talking

31

to him because he let me talk, and he asked a lot of questions. As I would walk home after my sessions, I would stop by the dollar store and steal something for my mom. She really liked those things that you could set on your TV or mantle to look at, so I grabbed some of those. Then I'd stop by the newsstand because the candy was at the bottom where you could reach it before the lady had to get up and bend over to see you. By the time she looked down, I already had plenty of candy bars, gum, and breath mints. My friends and I used to do this all of the time. They always took my candy bars because I was short, and they would push me down and throw the mints at me. But not today because they weren't around, and so they couldn't beat me up. "And what can I do for you little boy?" the lady asked me.

"My mom wanted to know how much is a pack of Pall Malls?"

She smiled and said, "You can't buy them. Tell your mom to come down here."

I just smiled and walked away as I stuffed my mouth fast and full of paydays. No, the lady wasn't coming after me, I was just greedy. My mom always said that I ate too much. "You'll eat one or two times a day," Mom would tell me. My last stop before going home was the grocery store. Now this was where I made the big money. I would stand outside and ask people for money to buy milk and bread, or I'd help them with their groceries. They would give me quarters, dimes, nickels, even dollars. But also there were people who knew my family, and everybody knew that my mom would not ask for nothing. So when they told on me to my mom or my sisters, I'd get in big trouble, but hey, my mom got her Pepsi and Pall Malls. She was happy, but she still might not feed me because she would say, "You should have eaten when you was out. Get in your room and shut the door." Sometimes I would leave it open just to make her mad, but Mom would slam it shut. I walked into the store and gave the lady the note. She looked at me and asked like she always does, "How old are you?"

"Seven years old." Then she would smile at me and hand me back the note. I always kept notes from my mom on me because if she ever sent me somewhere or said to go and get this for me without money, I could use my note to buy cigs or borrow the money. Every now and then I would have to change something in the note, cigs to milk, or pop to cigs, etc. Like I said, Mom showed me a lot, and I watched her, my uncles and my mom's friends. She turned around and said, "That will be $2.75."

"Please," I would say, "she also wanted a candy bar and two Pepsis."

"What kind of candy bar?"

"A Reese's, and that would be it. Thank you." As I held my hand out holding the quarters, she would say, "Here, I'll help you." She'd gather the change together and hand me the bag. Now I knew about quarters and how many it took to make a dollar, but I let her help me anyway. She was a white girl with blond hair and was pretty. I think the man who owned the store was her father. I wished I were older because I would have dated her. I had it made. I could do almost anything because my sisters didn't come up town that much, and Mom didn't leave home that much herself. She always sent me. I'm walking home down this hill to get to the apartment building. Teresa drinking my pop and eating my candy bar. Mom stayed across from Teresa. You would cut through this horse farm, jump the fence, and you were at my house. That was my way to get home, because in the summertime, apples grew on the trees, and I'd get me some to put in my room for later. As I came through the door, Mom asked, "Where have you been?" She snatched the bag from me and hit me with the stick a lot of times. I would hold my arms up so that she didn't hit me in my face. The last time she did that I really couldn't see afterward. I learned how to cover up my head and face and let my other body parts hurt instead. Mom opened the door after I had cried myself to sleep. "Adam. Adam, come here." Then she would explain, "Something could happen to you and I'd get in trouble. What is that damn doctor teaching you? I told them you're a thief and you're crazy as hell." I just stood there not saying nothing. Mom was drunk, and I didn't see anybody else in the room. The TV was off, and the record player was playing. I could hardly stay awake. Mom then said, "Come here." That meant come and sit by her feet, don't move, and hope that every time she raised her hand she didn't hit me. "You know those white people think you're crazy," Mom began. "That's why you go to that school for crazy people." High school and elementary kids went to school together, but they had special classes for kids who got into trouble. I had a couple people in my class that I thought was crazy. This one boy Darnell, he would throw chairs and hit teachers and the kids. He and his sister were there, but I never looked at myself as crazy. Mom went on to say, "He ain't no doctor, he is a shrink." I turned and looked at her, wanting to ask what that was, but she read my mind. "He is supposed to help you, but I told him can't nobody help you. You a lost cause." I don't know why, but every time after that, when my mom woke up she would kick me and wake me up. I was tired and hungry all of the time. I often went to bed without eating. Mom would just say that it would make a man out of me. Mom then said, "Tomorrow, I want you to tell him you can't see him no more."

"But next week is Christmas, and he said he got a present for me."

"That white man is lying to you. Plus I have one for you too." Now that was the lie. Five Christmases had come and go, but there was never a present for me. I just said, "Okay, I'll tell him." Friday was coming, and I had to tell my doctor that I wasn't coming to see him anymore. I liked him. We talked about everything at home, my sisters, brother, and my bedroom but I knew how Mom was, so I'd better had told him. I was on my way to school, and I was mad at my mom. I didn't want to quit. I was calling her a black bitch; I hated her. Why was she my mom? Why did I have to live with her? I wished she were dead. I was crying out loud, walking up the dirt road to school. Then out of nowhere a thought came. I'll go see this man who had this house uptown; he always needed something done. And plus, I'd seen my mom go to his office for something, I didn't know for what exactly, but I think he owned our house. I went to his house and knocked on the door. Nobody came. I decided to go down the street to his office. I didn't know his name, but I told him that I could come by today to make some money. He asked what I needed the money for. I told him so I could get my mom a present for Christmas. It was winter, and it was around Christmas, so he gave me some money. I left and went on to school. There were no buses for people who lived in the town. Only those who lived outside of town were allowed to ride the bus. So I walked to school, eating my candy bar with my torn tennis shoes and my worn-out coat that kept me cold no matter what. My mom had told me that men don't get cold, but my feet would be cold a lot. I made do with what little I had, for what I did have was mine. As I got to school, my teacher asked me why I was late. I told her I had to get some milk from the store. I knew the store opened at 8:00 a.m. because Mom used to send me all the time before it opened and before it closed. Like I said, my mom taught me things I would need when I got older.

"Adam," she replied, "please take your seat." All I could think about was going to work after school. Now I knew that my mom liked nice things, and when she was drunk, she would say to my sisters, "Look what your numb-ass brother got me. Y'all older and don't even think about me." And they would reply, "He stole it." Mom was mean, but when she'd been drinking, Mom would turn nice. I used to see my mom cry a lot when she'd been drinking. Then she would turn the music up so no one could hear her. Say she was sorry for the things in her life, she would go on, "Say, man, forgive me, I'm sorry" sometimes to me. I didn't know too much about school when I was younger because Mom kept me out a lot, and we moved a lot. So we were always in a new town and a new school. It was almost lunchtime, and I was hungry. Just then somebody came in to speak with my teacher. She looked up and said, "Adam, come here please." As I got up some of the kids were laughing at me. I kicked one boy because I knew two things, how to fight and how to steal. I knew if I hit him, they would see my punch, so I decided to kick him real hard. "Yes?" I asked.

"Your mom's in the office for you." I looked at her and she looked at me. As I walked out, I was scared. I didn't know why she wanted me, and my heart was beating very fast. Just then I saw her through the window of the office door. If she was smiling, that meant she was mad just being nice to the white people. But if she was not smiling, she needed me and her to go somewhere. I opened the door; Mom looked at me and said, "Hi. You ready?" I said yes and we walked out of the school. I asked, "Where are we going and what's wrong?" At this point in my life I was allowed to talk to my mom and ask certain questions without getting hit.

"We're going to see this man," she replied. I said okay, and we got into our brown-and-yellow station wagon. Mom started to speak, "You know I'm trying to help you, but you keep getting into trouble. I don't know what to do, but I know this man who can help you." I'm looking out the window of the car smiling. "What the hell is funny?" Mom snapped.

I looked over at her without a smile and said, "Nothing." Looking back out the window I thought to myself, I've never sat in the front seat and never with Mom on the other side of me.

I wasn't allowed to ride in the car. One time the car broke down, and my mom said that I was bad luck. From that time on, Mom and my sisters looked at me as bad luck, no matter what happened. We pulled up to a building, and Mom said, "Okay, we are here." I looked, and my heart started beating fast again. I asked if I could stay in the car, and she said, "No, get your ass out." I wanted to tell Mom that I was here earlier today, but I knew it would make her mad. I knew he was going to tell her, and I felt like I was going to pee on myself. "Can I go to the bathroom," I asked?

Mom said, "No."

"I need to go really bad."

"Hurry up."

"Okay," I replied as I shut the door behind me. I started thinking about what I was going to say to Mom after the man would tell her that I had already been here. She knocked on the door. "Okay, hurry up, boy."

"Okay."

My mom was loud in a quiet place and when I said we have to be quite she got louder.

I decided that if he said something to me about it, I would lie and say that it wasn't me. I opened the door and came out. I looked around the office to see Mom, but the only person I saw was the white lady who was there when we first came in. "You looking for your mom?" I nodded yes. "She's in with Roy and Tom. Just have a seat." She said something else to me about Christmas, and I just smiled and nodded my head yes. The door opened, and I could see Mom and the man. He looked at me and smiled and Mom said, "You ready?" I told her yes.

He said, "I'll see y'all later," and then shook my mom's hand. I stood there looking at them, thinking what if he were my dad. Now that would be nice because he had a nice car and a big house. He kept his hair combed and wore suits all the time. He wore glasses and had a small build. "Come on, boy."

"Bye, Adam," he yelled out. I waved my hand bye.

We walked to the car and Mom said, "I got some luncheon meat and chips for you. I knew it was lunchtime when I came and got you from school." As we were riding, Mom told me that she didn't know what they were going to say when she and I went to court next week. "I'm trying to help you," she pleaded. As we were riding, I started thinking about what the shrink and I had talked about during my sessions. We discussed how my mom hit me and didn't feed me, and how I felt about that. I knew something was going to happen in court, but I didn't know what.

I got picked up one morning on my way to school. Someone had called the police and told them that there was this little kid in the neighborhood knocking on doors. She was right, but I had also broken a door window to get inside a house, saying, "Hello? Hello?" That way, if someone came out, I wouldn't be scared, and they wouldn't shoot at me or something. I did what I normally do. I ate whatever they would have in the kitchen; I changed my clothes, shoes and coat. I took the food and clothes with me. Mom didn't feed me, and I never had good clothes or shoes. I used to cut my brother's shoes, coats, and pants just so my mom would give them to me because Troy was too good to wear messed-up clothes. She loved that boy and so did everybody else. Troy, Troy, Troy...Well, anyway, when the sheriff took me to the county-jail courthouse, they put me in this room with bars on it. He shut the door and said, "We'll be right with you. We have to get your mom." Now we lived in a small town, and everybody knew each other. The policeman knew me, but I didn't know him. The next thing I knew my mom came in and said, "What the hell you done now?" I didn't say nothing; I just looked up at Mom with tears coming down my face without a sound. Mom said, "Ain't no use crying now, you fucked up and now they're taking your dumbass away until court. Why were you breaking in houses and stealing mail out of people's boxes?" I still didn't say nothing. "Well, maybe where you're going you might learn something. Well, I'll see you in court." Mom turned and walked away. I called after her, crying and hollering loudly, but she didn't come back. That was it. I did live with her, but she didn't want me. I started kicking the door, banging and yelling. The man opened the door and said, "Adam, please calm down. I'm going to take you somewhere and get you some lunch. You'll be out of here soon."

I was crying, and in between gasps asked, "Can you leave the door open? I'm scared."

He said, "Yes. I'll be just around the corner if you need me." I sat on the bed and cried because my mom had left me here. I watch seasons go by, kids come and go, staff come and go, but not m—four years. I felt someone shaking me, saying, "Wake up, Adam, time to go." But I must have been dreaming because Mom didn't talk like that. As I woke up I saw this white lady bending over me, saying, "Adam, wake up." I sat up; I must have cried myself to sleep. And as I sat up, I felt that my pants were wet. She smiled at me and said, "We'll get you something to wear," and held out her hand for me to take it. I looked at her as she smiled at me, and I was thinking to myself, *Who is she and where did she come from?* I got up and asked, "Where are we going?"

She said, "Out of here. You don't have to be here anymore." As we walked out I was hoping to see my mom, but the only person I saw was the police officer at the desk, eating a half of sandwich. I looked away in a sad way. The police officer said, "Adam, here you can have it."

I said, "No."

He said, "You have to eat, you've been here all morning." I looked up at the lady who was holding my hand, and she nodded okay. I walked over and took it and said thanks.

He leaned over and said, "I'll tell your mom that you want to see her." I smiled and put the sandwich in my mouth and walked away.

The lady put me in her car. In the back seat were books or papers, so I thought she was from my school here to transport me back. I sat back on the seat, and she put the seatbelt around me. She said her name, but I don't remember it. She said, "We'll be there soon, and we can get you cleaned up and get something to eat. Would you like that?"

I said, "Yes," and then "Can I go home?"

She said, "We'll see." I looked out the window as we were riding to see if I could see where we were going. I didn't remember anything; nothing looked the same. She asked me questions like did I have brothers and sisters. I said yes. She asked how old I was, and I told her seven and a half. She said, "Oh, you're going to have a birthday soon." I said yes, but I didn't know my birthday because Mom never had or gave me a party or present. She said, "You can go out there and steal and get money. You don't need me to buy you nothing."

The lady went on to ask me if I liked school and what grade I was in. I told her I was in the third grade and that I liked school.

Then she pulled up to this big, big, big house. It was in the middle of all this green grass on top of a hill, surrounded by a tall fence made razor-sharp. I was scared. She opened the door, but I didn't get out. She said, "It's okay. I'll be right here with you."

The man inside the gate opened it and smiled. We walked on. As I was looking back at the man closing the gate, I started crying. Tears were coming down my face, but I didn't know why. Something inside of me just wasn't the same when I walked through that gate. As she opened the door, I pulled my hand away from her and said, "I'm scared." She said, "Don't be. It's going to be okay."

When I walked in, I saw kids' rooms with couches, chairs, tables, and a TV. There were big kids, little kids, a kitchen, and big eating tables. I started crying, pleading with her to take me home. She waved her hand to some man and said, "Would you take Adam to change his clothes and get him something to eat?" Taking me by the hand, he led me down the hallway through an unlocked door. As we walked in, he turned the lights on and asked, "What size are you?"

I shrugged my shoulders and replied, "I don't know." As we were in there he told me, "It's okay, we're going to help you."

"When can I go home?"

"We'll see" was his response. We went upstairs, and he took me into this big bathroom with a lot of sinks, toilets, and showers. He said, "Get dressed, and if you don't want those clothes just put them in the trash can and come downstairs." He handed me a towel, wash-cloth, soap, and toothbrush. I had never owned any of these things before. Back at home, I didn't get to brush my teeth, and I didn't have my own towel. As I was washing up I started crying, knowing that I wasn't going to see my mom again. I felt alone. I was scared now more than ever, but I wiped my eyes, showered, got out, and put my clothes on. I felt a little better just knowing that I was wearing new clothes. I came out of the bathroom and saw some kids walking down the hall. They looked at me and kept walking. It felt strange to be here because it seemed like I was living with a white family. There were no blacks around. I went downstairs and walked into this big dining room. There were books, games, papers, pencils, everything a kid could play with. "Hey are you the new kid?" this girl asked. I looked at her and shrugged my shoulders. She said her name and I told her mine. Then she said, "You'll be okay." I sat down and started eating my lunch at the table with some other kids. This man came by me and sat down and began talking to me. He said, "When you finish your lunch come down to the office."

I told him okay. He got up and asked one of the big boys to show me to his office. When I finished eating I stood outside his office and knocked on the door. I heard a voice say, "Come in, it's open." I looked both ways to see who was around. I was looking to see how I could run, but where? How do I get out? What door do I take?

How would I find my way home? "Hi, come on in." I looked up at him, and he was smiling. As I walked in he said, "Have a seat." He started asking me questions like if I knew where I was. "No," I replied.

"You're at a place called Sargetts Youth Center. Do you know why?" I told him no. He said, "They placed you here until you go to court." He asked me if I knew what I was going to court for. I said, "For breaking into some houses."

And he said, "Yes." Then we started talking about my mom, her phone number, address. How many people were in my family, where was my dad? Did I get beat on at home? Did I go to school? Then he started telling me about this place and how some kids were older than others. He explained that there were girls and boys here in different age groups, but that everyone had to stay with peers in their specific group. He talked about rules. "Everyone has chores, and everyone cleans up behind themselves." He explained what would happen if you broke the rules like fighting, stealing, or running away. You would get locked in a room until staff thought you had cooled down. Then it was time for a tour. He showed me the lockup room with metal doors and a small window to see out and in. Some rooms had one bed and others had bunk beds. There were some kids in one of the rooms yelling all kinds of things. He showed me where we played outside. There was a door leading out back where this big cage held a basketball hoop, swing set, and sandbox. It was a big playground with picnic tables and grass with trees all around just like a big rich home. There was a chain-link fence that went all the way around the playground. At the top of the fence were razor blades. He said, "Don't run away or you'll get cut by them." We went to the kitchen where he explained that we cooked our own food on the weekends. The kitchen staff was off. We went to the school located on the top floor of this big mansion. He showed me the TV rooms because big kids had one, middle kids, and then the younger kids. He said that the laundry was put in laundry bags with your name on them. Every person here was given seven pants, seven shirts, two pairs of shoes, seven underwear, seven undershirts, fourteen socks, one coat, one jacket, a lock for the footlocker, one raincoat and one pair of rain boots. "As you do good, you'll be able to go to the store. Everything you do here is on a points system. That's how you'll be able to go home, to visit or get out." He then showed me where I would be sleeping. We walked down to the second floor where the younger kids stayed. My room was big, and there were two bunk beds, and the beds were made up with pillows. There were toys, radios, dressers, closets. He showed me to my bed, and I set my stuff down. He said, "Now we're done with the tour. After you get out of school, you can watch TV until dinner.

I'll see you a little later." We went downstairs where he showed me to the organ room and said, "You can watch TV in here." I smiled and sat down on the couch. I was happy because nobody said I had to sit on the floor. As I turned the volume down on the TV, some kids came in laughing and talking. They said hi and I said hi. One of the boys asked, "Is this your first time here?"

I said yes.

He said, "I've been here twice. My dad drinks and then hits me. What did you do?"

I said, "I broke into a house."

He asked, "What did you break into your own house for?" With a smile on his face. I looked at him with a mean look.

I said, "I didn't live there."

He said, "Who lived there?"

I said, "I don't know."

"Well, why would you break into a house if you don't know them?" Then the guy came in the TV room and told the little boy to stop asking so many questions. The man who took me on that house tour came back, and I got up with the man and walked into this office and sat down. This lady started telling me the rules around the center, what I could do and things that I couldn't. Everybody plays and hangs out with kids their own age. Nobody under sixteen years old could smoke without parental permission. If you fought, stole something, or ran away, this would get you put in lockup. Every child was to go to school while here at the center. Everybody has study hour Monday through Friday from 6:00 to 7:00 p.m. Anybody caught sleeping, playing, not ready, or not doing their work would lose points and have to go to bed without a snack. There was a bulletin board out in front of the dining room that told you what your chores were. You earned points in everything you did, and you lost points when you did something wrong.

Points could get you a day pass, clothes, shoes, outside rec., walks, cigs, Friday to Saturday late-night movies, and weekend passes with family. As I was sitting there, I just kept thinking about Mom and what they may have been doing. Do they even know I'm not there?

"Adam, Adam did you hear what I said?"

"Yes!"

"Has anybody showed you to your room?"

"Not yet." She gave me two keys and said, "One key is to your room, and one is to your foot locker. Don't give or let anybody use yours. I'll show you to your room." We walked down the hall and up the stairs. I started seeing more kids with books in their hands, walking and talking to each other. Little boys were running all around with men telling them to slow down. Everybody was white; I was the only black kid I had seen so far. As we got to the room she explained, "They're getting out of school and getting ready for dinner, washing their hands, setting the table. Some kids are doing their chores. Some wait until chore time, which is at 5:00 p.m., 8:00 p.m., and in the morning at 8:00 a.m. You can stay in your room until dinner, or you can come down and meet the other kids."

"I'll stay here." As she shut the door, I walked over to the window that overlooked the backyard. There was a path leading out into the woods. Tears started coming down my face. I didn't know why, but I just wanted to go home. I was scared, I wanted out of here. I sat down on my bed and looked around my room. There were four beds with a dresser by each bed. There were four footlockers in front of each bed and a locker where each person could store his clothes, jacket, shoes, and coats. I didn't put my stuff in my locker or dresser. I put it all in my foot locker because I wasn't staying here, and Mom was coming to get me when I went to court. It was a weekday, and I was getting ready to go to court. I'd been in Sargettis for quite some time now. I was there about four years, and I was scared because I didn't know nobody. By this time, I had two new kids come and go in my bedroom. One boy went back home, and another boy got older and moved to another room because they keep you with your age group. You can talk to older kids, but you're not allowed to hang around them. I put my black pants on with my socks and shoes. Mike said, "You look nice, Adam."

I said, "Thanks." Mike was my roommate, and his bed was on the other side of the room from me. He was cool. We played cowboys and Indians together, ran and chased each other around the center. His mom and dad didn't want him, so they sent him here. His mom told him that she was coming to get him but never came back. He was eight years old, and he was my friend. They called him and me salt and pepper. You could get into trouble with staff if you got caught calling people out of their name, their race, or if you were having sex. "Do you think you're coming back after court?" one of the other boys asked.

"Yes, to say bye to my friend and to ask my mom if Mikey could come live with us." I put my shirt on, looked in the mirror, and smiled at myself, thinking that I've never looked this good and clean. I haven't seen Mom and my sisters and brother in a while but today I would be going home. Mike and I walked down to breakfast but I wasn't hungry. I just wanted some juice. The kitchen lady said, "Good morning, boys. What can I get y'all?"

"Nothing, we're having juice. My buddy Adam is going to court, and he's going to see his mom and get out," Mike explained. "Then I'm going to go live with my buddy."

She knelt down and looked at me and said, "It's gonna be all right. Just you wait and see." I stood there with the juice in my hand, smiling at the cook. "I'll make you a peanut butter and jelly just in case you get hungry." I knew it was early and I didn't have to be at court until 8:00 or 9:00 a.m., and I didn't have to go to school. Mike and I sat down at the table, and kids started coming down from school for breakfast. Now I knew a lot of the kids knew I was one year older than them, and a lot of kids knew me because I fought a lot, smoked, gambled, and liked one of the girls there. They were touching my shoulder, saying, "Good luck today."

Others rubbed my hair and said, "Good luck, fuzzy head," but I was looking for my real friend to come downstairs, so I could tell her something. I still hadn't seen her yet. Ms. Bernice would be coming soon to get me for court. This meant that she'd take you into her office and explain to you why you were going to court, how you should act, and where you would sit. If you were going to run, Ms. Bernice would put handcuffs on your feet and hands. I'd seen some people come in like that, and some had left the center that way. Everybody was telling me good luck, but I still didn't see my friend.

Ms. Bernice said, "Come here, Adam." I walked down the hall from the kitchen to her office. I liked Ms. Bernice, she wasn't mean. She looked real good and always smelled good. "Good morning, and how is Adam today?"

I said, "Happy and scared."

She said, "It's okay. You'll do fine today, and your mom will be there."

I smiled and said, "Do you think I'll go home today?"

She answered, "That will be up to the judge. You've been pretty good here, and that's what I'm going to say."

"Do I have to wear handcuffs?"

She looked at me and said, "No, where'd you get that idea?"

"I'd seen some kids like that."

Ms. Bernice replied, "I only handcuff kids who give me trouble. Are you going to give me trouble?" I shook my head no, and she gave me a hug and said, "I know. You are one of my good kids." As we were riding in the car, I was looking out the window wondering if Mom had quit drinking. Is she prettier now? Will she be nice to me? Will my sisters and brother be there? What is the judge going to say to me? Just then I said, "I don't want to see the judge. I want to go home."

Ms. Bernice said, "Honey, don't worry. Once the judge hears how good you've been, he might let you go home." When we walked into the courthouse, I started looking for my mom or somebody I knew, but there was no one. Everybody kept looking at me. We walked through these doors, and wow, just like that I saw Mom and Melvin, my mom's boyfriend. I ran over to Mom and was smiling. She asked me if I was okay. I said, "Yes and I like your clothes." Ms. Bernice said, "Okay, I need you two to get up front at the table." One thing I knew was that I was happy to see Mom and Melvin. The judge walked in and said good morning to everyone. At the table sat my mom, a caseworker, my shrink, and a teacher from my old school. Ms. Bernice and two old ladies also sat at the table. The judge started talking about why we were here. He explained that homes were broken into and bedrooms were gone through. Food had been taken, and windows had been broken. Then he went on to say how people's mail had come up missing. Witnesses had come forth saying they would see me opening mail and throwing things on the ground. As the judge was reading each offense, I looked over at my mom, and she was shaking her head. I looked at the people around the table to see what they where thinking, but they were watching and listening to the judge. He asked me was this stuff true, and I said I didn't know. The judge asked again, "Did you do these things?"

I just looked at him, too scared to say anything.

"You hear him talking to you, answer him."

"Yes, sir."

"Did you have help?"

I looked at my mom and she looked at me. I wanted to say yes, my mom told me to do it, but I told the judge no. He looked at me and said, "Everyone here knows Adam, and we're going to start with his shrink." He went on to say other things, but all I remembered that day was this, my shrink told them everything we had talked about, how my mom beat me and starved me. My teacher expressed that I would come to school late all of the time or not at all. "He steals kids' coats, shoes, lunches and bullies them for their money." Then one old lady explained how her home had been broken into. The other lady was someone whose mail I had taken. By this time I was mad, and everybody was looking at me. My shrink had told me that he would never tell anyone what we talked about in his office. He lied! The judge asked Ms. Bernice, "How has Adam been since he's been in your care?"

She went on to say, "He's a good kid. At first it took him some time to get it, but he follows the rules. Every kid sees an in-house counselor and Adam is doing well." Then the judge asked Mom if she had anything to say. Mom replied, "It sounds like y'all can get Adam to act right, go to school, and talk to y'all. Now I have six kids at home, I can't watch him all the time and my others. Every time I turn around the police is bringing him home, or I have to go to the school because Adam stole something or got in a fight. It's too much. Now that y'all have him, you deal with him, I'm not. Y'all took him, y'all keep him."

The judge asked Mom, "Are you sure of what you're saying here?"

She said, "Yes."

Everyone was looking down the table at Mom and me. Tears were coming down my face. Mom looked over at me and said, "That's your dumb-ass fault you're here. I told you to stay home that day. You are the one who said you knew where some money was."

The judge said, "Adam Johnson, I find you guilty of these charges, and you will stay at the center until you turn twenty-one years old, or until your mom moves out of the county." Everybody looked at me, and I looked at them as if to say, what did he just say? I knew I wasn't going home, so my tears started coming faster and faster. But just then Ms. Bernice said, "Judge, he's just a kid and you heard what kind of background he comes from."

"Ms. Bernice, I understand your concern, but the law has been broken. Now that's all, case closed." Everybody stood up except me.

Mom looked at me and said, "I'll tell everyone you said hi, and we'll try and come and see you." As she turned and walked away, I called my mom's name for what I knew would be the last time. "Mom! Mom!" but she kept on walking. I turned and looked at the judge, crying, with tears on my face. He looked back at me and said, "I'm sorry, son. I hope this is for the better."

Now back at Sargetts. I didn't listen to anyone anymore or follow the rules. I wanted to get locked up a lot. I didn't care anymore. People betrayed me; my mom didn't want me anymore. There wasn't no good coming out of this. The judge put me here until I turned twenty-one or until my mom had to move. She was not going to move because all of her family lived in Ohio, so I couldn't go home. There was no reason to get points anymore. I was sick. I didn't know what to do but be me, so every day I fought, stole, cussed, lied, and bullied without caring about the consequences. My friend Mike went home one day, and the girl that I liked, I just stopped talking to her and looking at her. Everybody had heard about me.

"If he bothers you, come tell us. His family doesn't want him." Some of the kids would tease me and say things like, "Don't nobody want you." "Somebody left a baby on the step."

They also said cruel black jokes as well. One day, I was about to eat lunch when three white boys walked over to me and smacked me upside my head. Now two years ago, I was scared of the older boys, but now, I wasn't the same little boy anymore. I told them to stop but they didn't. I got up, walked into the kitchen, got two frying pans, and started hitting the kid who hit me. The next thing I knew staff was pulling me off him. They put me in lockup until I cooled down. I don't know what they did to them, but I started yelling, "White trash." I was the only black kid here, and I started banging and kicking against the door. After that, staff found out that the other boys had started it, and it wasn't my fault. I did two days in lockup for cussing and fighting. It's been four years now, and I haven't seen Mom or my family. On visiting days, which were on Sunday, I would be good just in case Mom came. Every Sunday I'd sit in the TV room and wait. Monday through Friday, I waited for mail, or maybe even a phone call—nothing. Year in and year out, I waited. I stopped going to mail call, and I stopped writing, begging Mom to come. I stopped sitting in the TV room because I couldn't watch people be happy with their families. Some kids asked if I would be allowed to go on their home visits with them, but I wasn't. If something were to happen, they would get into trouble. I thought every-day about that courtroom and the people who were there on that awful day. I stopped trusting people and just depended on myself. The only person I talked to about anything was Ms. B. She knew what I was going through because she was there. Ms. B was nice to me. She would take me off grounds once a week for two hours and would ask, "What do you want to do?"

I would say, "Go home with you and never see this place again."

Ms. B said, "Your mom don't want you, but she won't let nobody adopt you. And I would have to quit my job to get you because we're not allowed to get involved while we work here."

I said to her, "Yes, you can. My mom sold me before to this man for a house and money."

She said, "That's terrible, what happened?"

It was Christmastime and my mom needed Christmas money. Her and the owner had been talking sometime about this. One day he knocked on our door and Mom said, "Adam, come here. You're going to live with him, and he'll be able to give you everything you need. Go get your stuff."

Lorri, my sister, ran up to me and said, "Where are you going?" I smiled and said, "With this man." She ran into the kitchen and, after seeing him, came back and said, "I know him. He's our landlord and he got money." I went to get my stuff, but the only thing was I didn't have nothing to get. We walked out the door and down to his car. I got in, and he asked me if I wanted something to eat. I told him no. I went on to explain to Ms. B how we spent the night in town, and then we headed out to his home at daybreak. I slept downstairs on the couch with the fireplace, watching the fire. I lay there thinking about everything, his kid, his wife, Mom, my sisters, and my brother. When I woke, I washed my face, folded the blanket, rolled it up, and then we left. It belonged to the man who paid for me. I don't know where he lived, and I don't remember his name, but the following details are what I do recall. When we got to his house it was nice. It was the best Christmas ever with a big tree and lots of toys. His wife was pretty, and his son was younger than me. We shared a bedroom, which was the first time I'd taken a bath, put on clean pajamas, and not slept on the floor. I was happy sleeping on a bed with clean sheets, pillows, etc. I was happy but sad too because I wanted to be home with Mom. Some tears. The next morning came, and they woke me up. It was Christmas. Christmas! I came out and sat down like everyone else to see what the family got. Mom would say, "That's Adam's and that's Troy's." But Troy would take all of the toys.

The dad said, "Adam, Santa brought you something too." I got a red, white, and blue football, clothes, a football stand holder, boots, trucks, and cars. We ate, played, and then I started getting homesick. I told the lady I wanted to go home. She asked me why.

"I miss my mom."

"But you live with us now. Don't you like us?"

"Yes."

"Well, why leave?"

I just kept repeating that I wanted to go home. The dad took me home after dinner; we didn't talk. Only thing he told me was that if I ever changed my mind, I could come and see him at his office. I thought my mom would be happy that I was coming back home. We stopped at McDonald's, and he asked me if I was happy with the presents. I told him that I was. I fell asleep in the back seat of the car. When I woke up I was home. I got out, got my stuff, and went up to the house. Mom opened the door. I was smiling. I saw my sisters and brother standing by my mom, looking at me. Mom asked, "What did he do now?"

"Nothing," the guy said. "He just wanted to come home. So after we talked about it, Adam still wanted to come home to you."

Mom said to me, "Is this true?"

I said yes.

Then Mom said to me, "Get your dumbass in here." When Mom shut the door she started yelling at me, "He paid for you. You don't live here anymore. Why did you come back?"

I said, "Because I missed you." Mom put me back in that same nasty bedroom. I thought she would be happy, but that wasn't true. I cried all night long. My mom gave Troy all of the stuff I had gotten for Christmas. Mom said she hated me and wished I would die. Only thing I knew was that I should have stayed with that man, but I really wanted to go home.

I wasn't afraid no more. Mom didn't scare me, and I was going to change everything. I was bad. I started taking things that belonged to other people like money and candy.

And I didn't care who told on me because I was mad now. I was eight years old at the time; my dad had left when I was five, and now my mom didn't want me. She sold me for this beat-up house with bad plumbing. My sisters were mean to me, and my little brother always lied to me and broke anything that belonged to me. Here I was sitting here in this kid's camp waiting on nothing because I knew nobody was coming to see me or get me out. One day I was in a bad mood, and my roommate was laughing at me, calling me dumb and dummy, so I ran over to him. I started kicking and hitting him, calling him names. Staff came running into our room. The boy was crying, and I was yelling and cussing. This was second shift, and they were kind of mean staff, so you had to watch what you said or did because they always put kids in lockup or sent you to bed without a snack. They wouldn't let you watch TV or play games. They even took away some kids' home visits. The staff person said, "I'm going to teach you a lesson. You're going to lockup." I started to yell and told them that it wasn't my fault. Both men picked me up and took me downstairs past the TV game room where people were sitting. The man opened the metal door, pushed me in, and said, "Let's see how you feel now about fighting." I was crying and pounding on the door. Then I heard this voice say, "If you keep that up, they will never come and see you."

I turned around and saw this tall white boy sitting on the bottom bunk. I was really scared now. I was only eight, but this boy was way older than me. I'd seen him around the house sometimes, but people always said he was crazy because he tried to run away. I didn't say nothing, but I now knew what staff meant when he said, "We're going to teach you a lesson." I got on my bunk, and the white boy was talking about something, but I didn't know what he was saying. After a while I fell asleep. The next thing I knew I was on the floor, with my back and head hurting from when he dragged me off the top bed down onto the cement floor. He was on top of me, saying, "Don't scream." He had his hands around my throat. "Or I'll kill you now." Not knowing what was going on, my mind started replaying my life. I thought about Mom, getting beat, my sisters laughing at me, my shrink, and being in court. Then I heard him say, "Open your mouth. You're going to suck this white cock. Open, open, you dumb nigger." That's when I opened my mouth because I couldn't breathe. He stuck his dick in my mouth. I was crying, trying to yell, but no sound came out. I bit down on his so-called dick like a carrot. He yelled real loud, punching me in the face and side. I bit down harder and harder. The light came on, and staff hurried over to me, yelling, "Let go! Let go!" The white boy was over top of me while I was on the floor. "Please let him go," staff cried, so I did. They pulled me up off the floor and put me in this other lockup room and shut the door. They said, "I'll be back to talk to you about this." I sat there trying to figure out what had just happened. I was just trying to sleep…The door unlocked and staff came in with some clothes. "Adam, I need you to come with me. I need you to clean up, and I have to see if you have cuts or bumps from this." He looked me over and said, "Your mouth is bleeding. Did he punch you?"

I said yes.

He replied, "Come on, we'll look at it."

We went into the bathroom. I was looking for that white boy, but I didn't see him nowhere. Now I was scared because I thought that he might come after me. It was third shift on duty now, and he asked, "What happened?"

I said, "Them dumbass staff put me in lockup with an older kid, and he tried to make me suck his dick. They said they were going to teach me a lesson." That's when I went over to the sink to look in the mirror because my face was hurting from the punches. I looked in the mirror and seen blood all over my mouth. I thought my teeth were knocked out.

So much blood, blood on my night clothes, hands, face. The staff person said, "Okay, I need you to strip so I can look at your cuts."

I said, "No, I don't trust y'all."

He said, "It's okay. We have to do this every time somebody gets into a fight." He looked over at me and said reassuringly, "It's okay."

I went into the shower, got in, and started crying. I didn't know why; it happened out of the clear blue sky. The man walked over and said, "I'm here until tomorrow. I won't let anything happen to you." I dried off, put my clothes on, went over to the sink, and looked at my face in the mirror. All of my teeth were still in my mouth. As I looked away from the mirror, I started thinking about him and what had just happened. I tried brushing my teeth, chewing gum, gargling, but that thought was still there. "Adam, I need to get you to bed because tomorrow you have a lot to talk about."

I said, "Okay."

"Adam, you will have to sleep in lockup."

I said, "No. I didn't do nothing."

"I know, but you and Tom got into it and I can't send you to your room. You won't be locked down, you will spend the night here in the open."

"What if somebody comes in?"

"They won't. The only person down here is you and me. You'll be okay."

I didn't trust him, but I knew he liked kids, and he was fair about everything. When morning arrived, they knocked on my door. It was open. I looked up, and it was Ms. B. I jumped up and ran to her with tears in my eyes. "Are you okay? I just heard about last night, but don't nobody know what happened until you tell us," Ms. B said. "Come on, we'll go to your room, so you can change and then have some breakfast."

We walked down the hall away from lockup. Ms. B said, "Nobody knows what happened but you." I looked at her, and she looked at me. Everybody was moving around, getting ready for school and breakfast. As Ms. B and I were walking, kids were looking at me all crazy faced. Some kids said, "Hi, Adam." "Good morning, Adam."

I didn't say anything; they had to know what happened. When we got upstairs to my room, Ms. B said, "Shut the door, get dressed, and brush your teeth." I sat on my bed with my pants and started looking out the window. Ms. B asked, "What's wrong?"

"I don't want to go downstairs because everybody's going to say I'm a fag."

Ms. B came over to me and knelt down and said, "What happened to you? Don't nobody know, and you're not a fag. You did what you thought was right."

I said, "Where is that boy?"

She said, "He ain't here—"

Then I asked, "When is he coming back?"

"We don't know yet." As Ms. B put her arm around my shoulder, we walked to the dining hall, and the cook lady leaned over to me and said, "How's my Adam today?"

"Fine," I said.

The older lady used to tell me all the time, "You're quiet" or "Do you have white in you?" "Your hair is soft."

"Do you want toast?"

"Yes."

"Juice?"

"Yes."

Then she said, "I heard Tommy was teasing you last night. Don't worry, Tommy will get his someday." All the staff was nice to me, and I think it was because they knew. My mom didn't come see me, call, or even write. I've been here two to three years, and I was the only kid who didn't get any mail, people to visit, or home weekend passes. Ms. B was my best friend; she was like a sister to me. I never had a mom who I wanted to be mine like I wished Ms. B was. She smelled good all the time, and she was nice to people. She was a social worker who actually cared. Ms. B said, "It's time for you to see some people about last night." I looked at her with a sad look. She knelt down at me and said, "I'll be right there with you." I walked into the office with Ms. B. I liked his office, the man who owned the center. He had a big black gumball couch and a big brown desk that shone when the sun hit. She must have known everybody there because everyone stood and shook her hand and smiled. Once everyone took a seat, I looked around. There were police officers present, the boss of the house, and some lady with paper and a pen. The man who owned the house sat with a suit on, black I think it was, and smiled at me. "Nice to meet you, Adam," he said. "My name is…" I don't remember what his name was, but he told me that they were all there to listen to me and find out what happened. I started telling them about what happened in that room. I explained to them that I was put in there because I got into a fight with my roommate, and I cussed him out. They asked what made us fight. I told them that he was saying things to me like I had no mom, or that I never got home passes and that I was dumb. Then staff came in and grabbed us apart. They asked who started it, and we both said each other. Then one staff took me by the arm, and the other staff grabbed my other arm and took me down to lockup. He said to me, "I'll teach you." I was hollering, saying I didn't start it, and that he was teasing me. They just told me to pipe down, unlocked this door, and put me in there with no light and locked the door behind me. I thought nobody was in there with me, and I started crying and yelling. Then I heard a voice tell me that they wouldn't come back that way. I turned around and saw this tall older boy sitting on his bottom bunk. I really started yelling then, "I won't do it again, please let me out." Well, the white boy was saying something, but I wasn't listening, I was trying to get them to open the door, but nobody came. I got on my top bunk and finished crying. The next thing I know I was on the cement floor with my back hurting and my head hurting with this big white boy sitting on my chest with his hand over my mouth. He was telling me not to yell, or he would kill me. I was sleepy, so I didn't know he was going to do that. Then he told me that I was going to suck his white cock. As I was telling my story, they all looked at me with their mouths open. I was thinking, why would they believe me? I was always lying or in trouble. I looked over at Ms. B., and she was wiping her face. I said to her, "I don't want to talk no more."

She said, "Adam, we have to hear what happened so that they will know what to do."

She patted me on my leg and said, "Go ahead." I looked around the room without saying nothing. The lady was still writing, and the officers were writing too. The head man was at his desk with his head hanging down in his hands. I didn't know what to say, I was scared. Every time I got scared, I would fight harder or go to the bathroom. I would ask to go every time my mom scared me. "Can I go to the bathroom, mom?"

He looked up at me and said, "Yes you can, but my name ain't mom."

Ms. B said, "Yes, sir. That's his mom's name."

The man said, "I'm sorry. Please go to the bathroom." Then he said, "Clean hands make a clean body." I smiled and walked over to the door and opened it. Everybody at the center was in school, so the halls were empty. The cooks were done until three thirty. At dinnertime there was always one cook present just in case. I sat down on the bathroom floor and cried quietly. I don't know how long I was in there, but I finally came out and went back into the office. I stuck my head in the door. "Come on in and have a seat." The head man asked, "Are you okay?" I nodded my head yes. He said, "Around here, Adam, you have to speak, okay?"

"Okay," I said.

"Are you hungry?"

"No, sir."

"Want something to drink?"

"No sir."

"Okay, now you were saying that he was on top of you?"

"Yes, sir, telling me what he wanted me to do."

"Then what happened?"

"He punched me in the mouth."

"How many times?"

I said, "I don't know, a lot."

"Okay, then what?"

Well, I went on telling them that I wouldn't open my mouth, and he threatened to kill me if I yelled. I was scared, mad, and crying. He hit me again. "Open your mouth, nigger. You're going to suck this white cock."

I tried to yell, and he stuck it in my mouth. I closed my eyes, balled up my hands, and bit down real hard. He started yelling. I knew I was winning because his hands let go of mine. I bit harder, and that was when staff came in and told me to let go. I had blood all over my mouth. They helped clean me up, and here I am now. The man said he was sorry that happened to me, and that I should have never been put in there with another person, and definitely not an older boy. "You had a bad night," the boss man replied after I'd finished talking. "I'll take care of this matter. Ms. Bernice will have you call home, and then we'll go from there."

Ms. B said, "Adam hasn't seen or heard from his family since he's been here. We tried to search, call, even go over there but she don't want to talk with us or Adam."

Tears were coming down my face. Then he turned and said, "I'll look into this. I promise."

I wiped my eyes and smiled and said, "Okay."

The officer told me that I was a brave kid because most kids don't say nothing. The woman who was writing walked over to me with her gold buff hair. She had a stale smell, with those black old woman shoes. She hugged me real hard and said something in my ears, but I couldn't hear her. She wiped her face and smiled at me. Ms. B and I held hands and walked out of the door. I looked back at the people in the office, and the head man said, "Don't worry, I'll see to this matter." Then he winked at me.

Ms. B said, "Now let's have some lunch, Adam. You and me."

I looked up at her and smiled.

I'd been at Sargetts for about three or four years now. I didn't keep count like some kids did. I'd seen girls cut themselves and kids run away because they'd been here too long. After some kids turned eighteen, they let them go even if they had no home to go to.

Everybody who worked there and lived there knew me, and they liked me. And I started liking them. I actually liked white people. During the week, we had class so what I liked most were Saturdays. We had no school and slept in until noon. We cooked and ate whatever we wanted. After we finished our chores, we could watch TV all day. You only had three to five staff members, two men and two women, on Saturdays and Sundays. We would make homemade pizzas for the movies on TV, and there was plenty of food and drinks. If you had an early bedtime, you didn't watch a movie or get to eat any pizza. If you got caught sleeping, staff would wake you and tell you to go to bed. Some people would tell on you just so they could nick out or have the whole couch to themselves. At this time in my life I was happy. I was clean all of the time, I had a clean bed, and I was eating good, hot food. Nobody was beating on me or making me do things I didn't want to do. I was in charge. I was beating people now. I wasn't a nine-year-old kid; I was a nine-year-old man. I had no family, just a mom and a dad who didn't give a damn about me. They only cared about the other kids they had. But now I was around people who cared about me. Ms. B used to write me once a week but never signed her real name, just from a friend. When I asked her if she wrote me, she would just look at me and smile. I knew it was from her because she knew when mail call came that I would leave the room. I didn't want nobody to see me cry. Another reason why I knew it was her was the smell of her perfume, the kind she wore on Friday afternoons for our one-on-one meeting. We both just smiled at each other, for this was our secret. Ms.

B. would also send me twenty dollars every Friday. I was going to school and cooking small stuff. I watched a bunch of kids go home or get sent off to other places. I have seen staff not come back. I've seen staff fighting the older boys; I knew of girls having sex with the boys and staff. I knew some staff who stole meat, money, clothes. I even had staff lie on me, but I never told nothing to anybody until that one incident. Life was good, and nobody knew about what had happened to me years earlier. I had so many points that I was allowed to do anything I wanted. Points were what showed how well you were doing. You even got points for saying good morning. But you could lose points for having a foul mouth.

I didn't want to leave because I was scared I might run into my mom. What would I do? I hated her, wished she was dead, but I still loved her with my heart. She didn't want me. Ms. B would take me off grounds for our one-on-one meeting. She said that I needed to get away more so that I could see things. Ms. B and I talked all the time, but on Fridays we could talk about anything. Sometimes I would talk about me living with her, or how long kids could stay at the center. She would say, "Don't worry, everything's going to work out for you." I learned how to play pool, basketball, and kickball. I learned how to play around with other kids. I never saw that white boy after that day, and my roommate eventually went home. He told me sometime later that if he had known my mom didn't want me, he would never have said that to me. Tommy had this baseball glove that I liked and desired to have. I couldn't play that good, but I liked hitting the ball and running around. But most of all, I wanted the glove because somebody gave him something, and I never got nothing. His dad gave it to him when he was six years old. I helped Tommy carry his stuff downstairs when it was time for him to go. Some of the kids and staff were down there waiting, and that was what we did when somebody went home. We waved and said goodbye. I looked at Tommy and said, "I'll see you sometime in life."

He said, "Yes, you will." He bent over and pulled out the black leather glove. I smiled as he handed me the glove. I said, "Your dad gave this to you."

He said, "I know, but now I'm giving it to you. I know how much you wanted it. Remember when I couldn't find it for two weeks, and then you said you had it. Losers keepers, finders weepers."

"Yeah but you found it in my locker." Then we shook hands and laughed as he walked toward the door. I kept that glove until I turned thirteen years old, and I never saw it again. Now summer came and went. Fall came and went. I was cool now; I was sneaking, smoking, and gambling. I had some girls there who liked me, but nothing ever happened because I was shy, and somebody always told on us. I was still getting letters from my friend Tommy. He wrote me for the last time to tell me that he wouldn't be writing anymore because his mom and dad were breaking up. All the kids at the center were afraid of me. The older kids made up stories about me to the new kids who came to the center. They would tell them that on Christmas Eve, I woke up and killed my family and put them under the tree. They would look at me scared or would say at dinner, "Hey, did he kill his family?" I would just smile.

They would say, "Yeah but don't say *kill* to him. He'll start punching you." Sometimes I would walk over to people and take over the TV, games, etc., etc., but it was fun and games. After being there for so long, you'd start telling lies too. We loved to see the look on their faces. Staff didn't tell on us, but they would come to us and say, "Not too much or somebody might get hurt." We would say okay and laugh. Christmastime was great with toys and getting to playing all day long. We took sleigh rides and drank hot chocolate. We didn't have to do nothing for most of the kids went home for the holidays or on a one-day pass. It might just be six to twelve kids left in the center. Even though I had some bad times, I did have some good times too. One day Ms. B said, "Adam, this will be our last time talking." I looked at Ms. B.

"What did I do? Was it the letters?"

"No."

"Was it when that boy hurt me?"

"No, Adam."

I didn't say nothing. I looked down at the floor, and tears started coming down my face.

I looked at Ms. B., and she had tears coming down her face. She looked at me and said, "Adam, your mom is coming to pick you up Wednesday at noon." Ms. B smiled and said, "Ain't that great?"

I said, "Hell no! She don't want me. Mom wanted to beat me for telling on her."

"Adam, I'm sure your mom ain't thinking about that. She'll be happy you're home."

I looked at Ms. B and yelled, "I'm not going with that mean-ass bitch!" I used to hear some of the boys say that about some staff women. I opened the door and ran out crying. People were asking me, "What's wrong?" "What happened?"

I ran to my room and cried, cried, cried. *Knock, knock.* "Adam, you wanted to go home didn't you?"

"Yes, but I didn't know it would be so soon."

"Adam, you've been away from your mom for a while. Maybe she's changed. Maybe she don't drink."

"But I want to live with you."

"Adam, we talked and talked about that. Now it's time for you to go home."

I looked at Ms. B and said, "I'm not leaving here. And if I go back to her, I'm running away." I put my head under my pillow. Ms. B rubbed my back, then she got up from the bed and walked toward the door. I looked up at her with my small brown eyes. "Do I have to?"

With her eyes looking at the floor, Ms. B said, "Yes Adam. And I will always think about you and love you." She turned real slowly toward the door, turned, and winked at me just like the head man did when he said he would take care of things. He did just like he said he would. Then the door closed, and I lay down with tears in my eyes. I knew it would be a long weekend because I was going to do something to stop me from leaving my new family; people who actually cared about me. Now Mom wanted me back. What is she broke or did she need me to look for clothes? What, did she want to beat on me? Oh I know, she needed me to steal for her. Whatever it was, after this weekend they would not let me go home. I'll burn down my room. No, no that might hurt somebody. I know, I'll break in the office and mess it up. No, no I'll get in a fight and then she would have to wait until they decided to let me go. I had a plan, now I needed the who and where because I got along with a lot of the kids. Monday came, and I got dressed, ate breakfast, and waited for the boss to come in before Ms. B. He always came in first because by noon he was gone until the next day. "Hello, Adam, how are you doing?"

"Good, sir."

"Are you ready for your big week?"

"No, sir."

"What?"

"No, sir. I don't want to go home, she don't want me. I haven't seen her since court. She didn't write or come see me."

"Adam, I can understand why you're upset, but it's time for you to be with your family."

"I don't know them, I know you."

"We care about you too, but we don't stand in the way when it comes to family.

Whatever you need I'll help you, money, and clothes, pick you up one weekend, whatever just tell me."

"Don't let her take me."

He walked over to me and gave me a big hug and said, "It's just Monday. I'll look into what you're saying about your mom." Then he smiled and patted me on the head and said, "I'll see you later." Now I knew I was going home and should be glad, but what was I going to…beatings every day, kids that I didn't know and most of all, kids that didn't care about me. My mom loved to drink. At least here you didn't get beat, the staff doesn't drink and mostly all of the kids liked me. I knew he was going to send me home, but if I could just come up with a plan…that would be all I needed. "Adam, time for school." I got up off the couch and grabbed my books with a small smile on my face. One of the girls asked me, "Why are you so happy today."

I smiled and said, "Now that I see you, I'm happy." I couldn't tell her my plan, or she would tell on me. Class seemed extremely long today. I couldn't find nothing that would get me into trouble. It seemed as if they knew I was leaving, and everyone was especially nice to me. Well, maybe at lunchtime something might happen. A building fire would be nice, or perhaps I would fall and break my leg. It was lunchtime, and Ron walked up to me and said, "I overheard one of the staff say there is a big surprise for somebody at lunch." I smiled really big. Something was going to happen today, and I wouldn't go home and I could stay. Before lunch we could go to our rooms and get ready. We always had cold cuts, pizza, fries, hamburgers, and juice. I liked all of them, and we ate really well. I knew if I went home, all of that would stop. I washed my hands, ran downstairs to the kitchen, and there it was a nice hot pizza with cheese. I put my hand out to get it but just then Ms. B came in and said, "Adam, can I see you please."

I looked at her and said, "Yes, ma'am." I put my plate and tray back and went with Ms. B. We walked into her office and she said, "Adam, I like you as if you were mine, but I'm not going to be here this week. I wanted to give you something before you went home."

I said, "I'm not going home."

She turned to me and said, "Why?"

"I talked to the boss, and he said that he would look into it."

She smiled and said, "Yes he will, but your mom wants you to come home now." Ms. B pulled out this bat and a new baseball glove.

"Wow, is that for me?"

"Yes, it is." I ran over to her and gave her a hug. She hugged me back, and for the first time she kissed me, really kissed me. I was happy. No one ever kissed me before, and now Ms. B had kissed me on my cheek. I smiled and said, "Thank you! I'll never forget this day."

"Now you go and eat your lunch." So I skipped down the hall back to the kitchen, smiling all the way. Everyone was at the dinner table, eating lunch. I walked in with my two pizzas and juice. One of the staff said, "Well, look who came to lunch, Adam." Everybody clapped, and I stood and took a bow and said, "Just money please."

Everybody laughed because if you were the last one at lunch, somebody would say something smart. The staff said to everyone, "Please, after school, put your stuff in your rooms then come downstairs to the dinner table. There's something the staff would like to say."

Ron looked at me and said, "I told you."

And I said, "Yep." I was happy. I had pizza and I'd gotten a baseball glove. As I sat in class looking out the window, I watched the leaves blowing away and wondered what it would be like to be a leaf. It could fly anywhere it wanted. It had no boss, nothing just free, free, free. "Adam, did you do your math last night? Adam, are you listening to me?"

"Oh, yes ma'am. I was just looking out the window at the trees." I liked her because she always said something positive no matter what was happening in your life, or who you were. She told me I was going to grow up strong like a tree. There was this boy in class who played around and joked a lot. She told him he would be a comedian. She always knew what to say to us when we were down and feeling sad. People kept me happy and laughing all day today for some reason. Looking back, I didn't know that people could care about someone as much as they did for me. "Yes, I did my homework."

"Would you please bring it to me?" Walking up to her desk, I could feel something, but I didn't know what. I wasn't sick, I wasn't hot or cold, but I felt good, happy. Why? I wondered. I didn't want to feel like this. This was how you felt when you were going back home with your family. All of the kids used to talk about things like this the day before they went home, and now I'm having a turn. Why? Who cared, they wanted me! I didn't want them. As I put the paper on her desk, she said, "Adam, I've enjoyed you in class. Keep up the good work." I smiled at her and went back to my seat. I heard someone call me teacher's pet, but it didn't bother me. People knew not to fuck with me. I'd beaten kids up before, and the rule was don't tell and you'd be okay. Even I lived by that rule and if that white boy wouldn't have hollered, maybe the staff wouldn't have come because I was not going to snitch. I was a man who handled his own. That's what my mom always told me to do. I thought about my mom a lot and my family, but I was mad at them. They didn't even write me. My sisters were older than me, and they knew what happened to me. I've asked myself so many questions that I stopped thinking about it. I played as much as I could. I was strong now, older, not some pee boy whose mom beat him all of the time. I'd seen things in life now, and Mom couldn't just hit me anymore or make me steal things. When I first came here, I stole and lied, then I started acting better. No more stealing, and no more lying. If I couldn't speak some words, staff would help me. I learned how to cook, clean, and make my bed. I knew how to do these things from my mom, and those were the things I made points on. Kids didn't like cleaning or making their beds. I was disrespectful to staff, kids, everyone because Mom didn't want me, and I hated everybody who wanted to help me. After two and a half years there, I started learning and listening to staff. They spent extra time with me, telling me how much they cared about me. At this point of my life, self-esteem was low. Everybody knew my mom didn't want me, and I was there for stealing mail and breaking into homes in the rich neighborhoods. Some people knew why I was there, but I never told the new ones who came in after me. The kids who knew called themselves helping me out, so that I wouldn't go off on people. I used to go off, just hitting and punching. I spent a lot of time in my room, not watching TV or going to the store down in the basement. I stayed on punishment, so they taught me how to act around people. They showed me how to eat slowly instead of fast, how to talk to people, how to wash myself and how to read better. I was in a new life, and now Mom wanted to take it away. How can this be?

Our school was on the other side of the building. It was just some classrooms with teachers who came in from the state to teach us. We knew what to say and what not to. Some things could get you sent away for touching them in the wrong place or saying vulgar things and some things got us locked in solitary or points were deducted. The teachers seemed more like social workers. They all talked soft, nice, and they ate with us at lunch. Then we went outside for recess. We changed classes twice throughout the day. School started at 9:00 a.m. and ended at 4:00 p.m. This happened so that some kids could talk with their social workers while others went to school. Everybody had a social worker; if you had problems with someone or staff or yourself, they wanted to know. We had two hours to go before school was out; it was almost over. I would hurry downstairs, so I could get a good seat. Sometimes when they wanted to talk to us they played some type of game. Under your chair you might win this, or you could have a pass for a day. I wanted to win something this time. I was little but I was fast. Whenever we played sports, everybody wanted me, fast Adam. I loved to run. For a while they wouldn't let me outside because they thought I would run away. I had to prove myself to staff before I could go outside. When I first got there, I didn't follow any rules, but now life was good. Life was good, and now it was time for me to go home. As everyone started coming downstairs, staff entered the dining room. The head boss was there. Ms. B was there. The cooks, some from second and third shift, were there as well. Now I knew something was about to happen because whenever the cooks came, that meant it was somebody's birthday or something had happened within the center. I started looking around the table wondering whose birthday it was or if somebody had pulled the fire alarm. Did somebody run away today? "May I have every-one's ears and eyes?" The boss man always said that so people would stop talking. He didn't like people talking or looking around while he was speaking. He said it showed a sign of weakness. "The reason I called everyone here tonight is that the center has some good news. We are pleased to announce that Adam is going home Wednesday." People started clapping, crying, shaking my hand, hugging me. Then he said, "We want these last hours to mean something to you. So no more chores and no more school…unless you want to say goodbye to your teachers." Now as he was talking, I was thinking, they are kicking me out just like my mom did. Or is it my time to go like everyone else. "Adam, what do you want for dinner?" That was the head cook. Everyone was quiet. I looked around at everyone, and they looked at me. Whenever someone had a birthday or was going home, you could pick dinner and a drink, but you had to eat it. One time this boy said he wanted breakfast food for dinner, then he didn't eat it, and some people followed him. The rule was don't get it if you're not going to eat it. My mom would say, "Your eyes are bigger than your stomach."

I looked at the cook and said, "Nothing because I'm not leaving with those people."

Then I ran upstairs to my room crying. I'm not leaving here. Minute by minute went by, and I sat on my bed looking out the window. There was a light rain falling down outside. I was thinking about running because I was allowed outside, but I was scared. I was far away, and where would I go? I didn't know where Ms. B stayed. *Knock, knock.* "Adam?" I heard a voice outside my door. "Adam, may I come in?" I wiped my eyes on my sleeve. "Yes, the door is open." That's what staff would say. It was the head man. "Adam, I'm sorry all of this is a shock to you, and we all will miss you." He started talking about the time I first came there and how young I was, and he didn't know if I would make it. All of the fighting, not getting along with my peers, and calling people out their names. And of course he mentioned some of the bad habits I used to have. The boss man always gave us a pep talk. He showed us that he cared because he grew up in foster care and came back to help kids like me. "But as time went on," he continued, "I said to my staff, give him a chance, he'll come around and you did. Now you're a young man, and you've learned lots of good tools you'll need later in life. People just can't take advantage of you anymore. You're no longer that six-year-old, small, skinny kid. You're bigger, stronger, older, and taller." He looked at me and smiled, and I looked and laughed. Then I said, "I'm still short."

"Yes, but with a mind." We all called him the boss because he knew what to say, how to get things done, and he was true. "Now you have to hold your head up, keep your mind on time, and go downstairs and let the cook know what's for dinner. I'm starving."

I looked at the boss and said, "For real?"

He smiled and said, "Yes." The boss never stayed. He always said he had to go, but here he was staying for my dinner. I ran downstairs into the stainless-steel kitchen, shouting, "I know what I want! I know what I want!"

"Calm down. Calm down, Adam. What can I make you?"

"Chili dogs, chips, and fries."

"Okay, that sounds good. Now go and let everyone know."

"Okay," I replied but I was shy. I just ran away crying. I walked into the dinner area with my head down and said, "We're having chili dogs and fries." When I looked up, there were more people there, and this time, there were gifts on the table. One of the kids walked up to me and said, "I wish I was going home."

I smiled and said out loud, "I'm sorry for running off."

One of the lady staff came over to me and said, "It's okay. We just love you so much. We want you to be happy no matter where you are." She hugged me and I hugged her. I looked over at my best friend, Ms. B. She gave me the thumbs-up and I did the same. I was still sad and mad because I was leaving all of the people I cared about. That night, before I went to bed, I said my goodbyes to the third-shift staff with tears in my eyes.

They fed my heart with a lot of love to take with me. I wasn't so hard after all. One of the female staff said, "You was hell coming in but an angel going. May God enrich your life wherever you maybe." Forty years later, I can still feel and hear those words till this day.

I couldn't sleep that night, because when I woke up the dream was over. A woman beating me and saying you ain't shit, and laughing. I lay there wondering, will she hit me? Is my little brother bigger than me? Does he still lie on people? Is my mom going to make me steal again? I hadn't stolen nothing in three years or been in a fight in over two years. I didn't cuss unless you made me mad, but I was still scared of Mom. I didn't want her beating me anymore. What if she did? Would I fight her? What if she told me to go get her a pack of cigs? People here smoked but I didn't. I tried it, but it didn't work for me. How was I going to tell my Mom, "I'm not getting you none." She would pick something up and hit me with it. She's put the heels of her shoes in my head, hit me in my ears, and burned the bottom of my hands when I got caught stealing. She'd broken my leg before, knocked my arm out of socket, starved me, spit on me, and sold me. She'd kicked me out of the house to look for her boyfriend. She's kept me home from school. Now I'm bigger, faster, smarter, stronger, and some say I fight like a lion because I don't stop until my prey is lying on the ground. Whatever it took to win, I did it. My roommate heard my cries, and he called my name and said, "Adam, are you okay?"

I didn't answer at first, but then I said, "Yes. I just don't want to go home...I don't know them. I know they're my family, but I haven't been around them in four to six years."

"Adam, you and me been here for sometime now but you longer. I've seen you handle yourself good. And no matter what happens, I know you'll deal with it. So quit worrying and get some sleep. You have a new day ahead of you."

I liked my roommate. He had a black dad and a white mom. He was there because he hit his principal for calling him a yellow monkey. He was twelve, and I was eleven and a half going on twelve. If I was doing something wrong while he was around, he'd run up to me and say, "Little brother, don't be like them white kids. Have some respect about yourself." Or he would say, "You will be a great man one day and they might need you." He was a good friend to me, and I hope I was to him. "I'll just wait until tomorrow and see how I feel in the morning. Good night."

"Good night." As the night passed, I was getting scared or my nerves were just bad. I kept waking up crying, feeling sad, but I thought that I should feel happy and full of joy. I wasn't, I was scared. I must have finally gone to sleep because when I woke, my roommates were gone. I jumped up saying, "I'm late. They're going to take points from me." That's what happened when you overslept. You'd lose like 250 points or something like that. If you wanted to get away for a couple of hours, it would cost you 25,000 points, and you would have to be on level five to six. That level meant you were almost done with your goal sheet and the program. No one woke me up, and I normally didn't sleep hard. My roommates did say that I snored really badly. They used to wake me up until I told them that I would cut their hand off if they touched me. So they started using earplugs. Wait, I told myself, today is my day. I remembered this as I sat down on the bed. No, no, not today. God, I'm not ready. I finished putting my clothes on, so I could go down for breakfast to face my worst nightmare. But why, God, why me today? How come some other person couldn't go home today? There were other kids who needed to leave and go home. As I opened my door, I looked around just to see where I'd been for the past couple of years. I couldn't believe I was leaving. I hoped to stay until I was grown. I wiped my eyes and said, "I love you," I said to Ms. B. "Wow. I can't believe you made all this for me."

The cook said, "Adam, I remember the day you came here. Ms. B brought you into the kitchen and said, 'This is Adam.' He will be staying with us for a while. Would you make him what he wanted? I asked you what your favorite food was, and we both said French toast, eggs, bacon and then laughed." She always made sure I got enough to eat.

I asked, "Why didn't anybody wake me up?"

She said, "I asked your roommates where you were, and they said that you had a rough night. And they told staff. I was told to let you sleep, seeing how you're leaving today." I lowered my head and said, "Yeah, don't remind me."

"It's okay, your mom will be proud of you. Things have changed in your life since I've met you. Eat up. I made this just for you."

Wow, just like I liked it. White powdered sugar over four French toasts with lots and lots of syrup, scrambled eggs on one plate with my bacon. Good, almost done but not crunchy and with a glass of orange juice. "Thanks, I'll miss your good cooking."

"Hey, I'll make you a goodie bag with some sandwiches okay?"

"Okay." She patted my head and walked away. She was nice, and if I had to guess her age, I would say thirty years old, married with one kid. She was a white female with blond hair and real smooth skin. As I was putting away my dish, Ms. B walked in and said, "How's my Adam?"

"Not good at all."

"I know. I heard you had a long night."

"Yes, ma'am. Do I have to go?" She sat down with me at the table and explained to me why I should leave with my family. The next thing I know I was waiting for my mom. I am sitting in the hallway. Maybe she ain't coming. Maybe her car ran off the road, or maybe she ran away. I wanted my mom to see me now. I had new shoes, new clothes, my hair was combed, teeth clean. She would be happy. Maybe she'll hold her arms out for me and tell me she missed me, and my sisters will be happy to see me and my little brother. I had so much stuff to take home, but where would I put it? Did they still live where we did? If so, I'm not putting my things in that room. I'm not going to sleep in there. I started worrying about my clothes. Will my brother bother them? I don't like people touching my stuff. I broke his nose. The last time I've seen him. Where will they let me sleep? I don't sleep on floors anymore. Thinking about that, now I really didn't want to go back. As I was looking out the window, I heard this voice say, "Adam." I looked up and there she was, just like I remembered my Mom. Small, little, thin, dark skinned with her hair pulled back with a wig on and those big eye glasses on. "Hey, come give your mom a hug." Most kids run to their parents but not me. I couldn't move. Was this Mom or a look alike? I never remembered her with a smile or being this nice. I walked over to her. I saw some of the staff peeking around corners and through the doors. The only person allowed around at this time was your social worker to give a report to the head man. He would sign off on the papers allowing you to leave. No one had seen my mom or knew what she looked like. Ms. B said, "Adam, give your mom one of those big hugs from the hills." My mom looked at her as if she had stolen something. I gave my mom a big hug. The boss stuck his hand out and said, "Hi, my name is…" I can't remember his name. Then Ms. B said, "Hi, I'm Adam's social worker. I've worked with Adam since he's been here. Now let's step into the office to get this process started." We went into the office, sat down, and started talking. They let my mom know how I had grown over the years and handed over some records of my schooling and health. They told her about what had happened to me a couple of years ago. She looked at me and the boss and said, "If he's gay I don't want him. He's already making me move." We all looked at one another. Mom went on to say, "The only reason I'm here is because y'all people keep sending me letters, calling my phone, coming by my home, telling me to come see him. I told you people before you got him, you deal with him. I'm only here because I'm leaving, and y'all told me that I had to come get him. Are you ready to see your sisters and brother?"

I nodded my head yeah. As I was about to walk out the door, I stopped and turned around and saw all the people standing there watching. I ran back. Not to Ms. B or the cook. Not to the other staff, nor the kids. I ran to the person who helped me the most and cared about me, I ran to the boss. He knelt down and gave me a hug, and all the people crowded around me. They hugged me and kissed me and said how much they would miss me and how they would tell every kid about me. I ran to get my things and started walking into my new life. "They must really care about you."

I smiled real big. "Yes, they do, and I love them." Two things my mom hates, white people and my smile because it reminded her of my dad. But people have told me that I have a nice smile. So I knew she didn't like that. When I walked out, I saw this light-skinned man and four girls. There was a boy there seven or eight years old. They walked over to me and said, "Adam, you know who I am?"

"Yes." Lorri the oldest, Lisa, Tammi, Olivia, Troy, and Melvin. Everybody was saying bye. I got into this brown and green station wagon with the seat in the back where you could look out the window at the cars in back of you. I waved out the windows at the people for the last time. Everybody was looking at me. Then my little brother said, "Mom, he crying. He crying." I looked at him and just for one moment, he almost got punched in the mouth for talking about my family. I didn't play that. I was a pretty serious kid, and I didn't play too much with kids. My mom stopped that stuff when I lived with her. I hated so much that I did not like playing with people at all. But this is one of the things I learned how to do while I was at the center. Well they started teasing me saying things like, "Those white people got you looking good, new shoes, clothes."

Lorri said, "You look good." Troy was going through my bags.

"Get out of there. Ain't nothing in there of yours. Get out, please."

"Look, he got manners now."

"Look, nigga, I didn't want to come and get you, but Lorri said we couldn't leave you, so don't forget I could have left you there."

I didn't say nothing. I just watched my brother get out of the backseat with me and sit with the girls. I didn't care anyway. He was soft. I would have gotten someone to kick his ass if we'd stayed back at the center. I already hated them, but I didn't say nothing. I just listened to what they were talking about. I pulled out this game or something and that's when the same old shit started. Troy snatched it out of my hands and I grabbed it back. "It's mine, not yours," I said.

He kept on saying, "Give it to me."

"Give that to your brother. You haven't seen him in a long time."

I said, "But this is mine, not his."

"I don't give a damn." My mom cussed so much, you would think that she was a man. I gave it to him because she probably would have hit me. Mom asked us did we want some food. We said yes. I said, "I have my lunch, they packed me one."

"Oh, now you're too white to eat with us?"

"No," I said.

"Shut your dumbass. Can't you see they brainwashed you. You're not white, so stop talking white."

I kept telling them, "I'm not white."

"I didn't tell you to talk." I looked out the window, and tears were coming down my face. I wished I was back at the shelter, my true home. I started thinking about how the TV rooms were different colors. Each age group had their own room to sit in. What were they doing now? Who came in and took my bed, and how was Ms. B doing? I knew it hadn't been that long since I had been gone but I didn't want to leave there. So I was tired I just, lay down.

When I woke up, they were eating. I sat up and they looked at me. They were eating chicken and hadn't even asked me. I opened my brown bag. Wow…what was all of this? They gave me some good stuff. As I looked into the other bags, there was even more stuff. I saw some paper; I looked at it but didn't know what it said, so I put it in my pocket. My reading wasn't good, and I needed some help with some words. I was in the sixth grade and eleven years old. I was 4'5", weighing 90 to 110 pounds of solid muscle. I did sit-ups and push-ups before I went to bed every night for the past three years. It made me stronger and helped keep me in shape. Just because I was short, people liked picking on me, so I had to show them that I was not afraid. It did not matter how big that person was either. "Boy, you're black and you're bad luck. That's all you will ever be." I opened the foil and there it was, my peanut butter and jelly on toasts. I liked that because it made the peanut butter and jelly taste better. Mom said, "Look at this shit. They even got him eating like he white."

"Look I'm not white, I'm black." We were at one of the car, truck stops. Melvin was working on the car; Mom was smoking a cigarette and cussing Melvin out. Troy, Olivia, Tammi and I were playing. Lorri and Lisa were together. I clearly remember Troy throwing my football in the river. I hit him, and he ran to Mom and told on me. She said, "When we get to the city, I'm going to call them and tell them to come get your black ass. You're not going to come back beating up my kids."

"Good, I don't' want to be here anyway."

She made me go sit in the grass with my back against her. I stopped and looked at her.

"What, them white folks tell you don't sit on the ground." I just stared at her, thinking how come you're not dead. I don't like you. As I was standing there daydreaming, I didn't see Mom get up until I felt her hit me. Before I knew it, I said, "What the fuck you hit me for?"

"What did you say, nigga?"

I started backing up. "Nothing."

"You goddamn right you didn't say nothing. Get your ass in the car, in the back seat and sit your black ass on the floor, not on my seats. Now let's see what them white folks say now."

I cried as they laughed and pointed at me. I was pissed. She gave my toys, games, and clothes to Troy. Everything I had she took from me that fast. "Shut that shit up. Don't nobody want to hear you cry." I didn't say a word. I sat quiet and scared with my arms around my legs. I didn't know what was next, I just knew I started seeing flashbacks like at the center when I was asleep. I would wake up crying saying, "Stop, Mom, don't hit me," and my roommates would wake me up.

"Do anybody have to go to the bathroom?" We stopped, and everybody got out of the car. Mom told me to stay until they came back, so nobody would steal our stuff. There were clothes everywhere in the car. I said, "Yes, ma'am."

"Stop that shit right now," she would say, "I'm not your damn ma'am."

I remembered the boss kept me downstairs to talk to me while my mom and Ms. B put my stuff in the car. He said, "This is yours. I want you to hold on to it. I was to give it to the parent, but I don't think you'll see it. Here, put it in your pocket and don't tell anyone." I reached in my back pocket, pulled out the envelope and opened it.

"Wow," I said out loud. I got up to see if anyone was coming. I looked again. There were ones, fives, tens, twenties, fifties, and hundreds in the envelope. I closed it fast, took my shoe off, and put it in there so nobody could find it or take it. I was happy. I was not going to tell Mom. Here they come. "Get out and hurry up before we leave you." As Melvin opened the back of the station wagon, I ran out to the bathroom, hoping and praying that they would leave me. I'll be okay, I've got money. I knew I had money, but I didn't spend it because I never went anyplace. They gave us money for birthdays and Christmas. Families sent kids money, but mine just added up and up. I didn't think it was this much. I counted it, five hundred dollars. Yes, five hundred dollars. I might not read good, speak good, or pronounce words right, but I knew how to count money. My teacher said I was good with numbers. I put two twenties in my pocket in case we stopped at the store. When I came out, the car was running. As I walked toward the car, Melvin started to pull off slowly. I started running, while my family was laughing. Even I started laughing. I ran, then I ran faster, and I outran the car. "Wow, how did you run so fast?" Troy asked me.

"I'm Big Brother, I can do anything."

"You can't fly."

"No, but if I have to I will."

Mom said, "That's my Adam. Boy, I didn't know you can run like that."

I yelled out, "Yes, ma'am."

Everybody started laughing, saying, "He called you ma'am."

"I know. I told him to stop that shit, I ain't white."

I asked Mom, "Where are we going?"

She said, "Far away where those damn white folks can't bother me anymore, or talk about your sorry ass. We're headed to Columbus."

"I never heard of that before."

"I know you haven't, nobody has."

Lorri said, "Melvin's sisters and brother live there. They said it's nice, big lights, lots of cars, people."

Tammi said, "I can't wait."

Tim said, "Me too. I'm tired of riding in this car. I can't wait to stretch my legs."

"Get back there with your brother."

"No, he's weird."

I didn't care; I had the whole back seat to myself. The more he talked, the more I disliked him. He was still spoiled, even more so now. While I was locked away he took my spot.

It seemed like we were never going to get there. We stopped to get Mom some beer and Melvin some wine and us some candy. Everybody got out. "You stay."

"Why," I asked?

"Because you steal."

"No, I don't. I haven't been to a store in four years." They looked at me as if I had just shot somebody.

"Four years?"

"Yes."

"Well, that don't mean shit. You can steal other things."

I went back to the back of the wagon mad as hell. I called my mom everything except her name. I wanted to see how stuff had changed. I had seen black women with white men. I even saw black people working in stores. We'd passed a McDonald's and a Wendy's. I couldn't believe that she was doing this to me. The next time we stopped, I was going to tell her that I had my own money. When they came back, Tammi asked, "You still like those Reese's cups?"

I said yes.

She gave me one and said, "Welcome home." Tammi was mean to me when I played house with her and didn't do what she told me. Other than that, we were the same. Same age, and we had dark skin. She was one year older, dark skinned like me, with long black hair.

She was smart in school. It wasn't so bad now; I guess they had to warm up to seeing me. Mom said, "We have to stop at a rest stop because Melvin is drunk, and he can't drive like that." Mom was talking crazy to Melvin, and we were trying to catch lightning bugs to make rings out of them. I learned that while at the center. We were laughing and playing.

They asked me all kinds of questions like was I gay and did I get beat up. Did I think about them? Who were my friends in there? Did I know anyone before I got there?

How was the food? I just told them the truth. "I don't steal, and I don't lie anymore.

They were the best people I have ever known. They were my family, and that is what we were taught."

"So now you think you're better than us?"

"No, not better but wiser now. People just can't say anything to me."

"I'm your mom, and I will always tell you what to do."

I stopped talking because Mom was getting mad, and I was talking to my sister Tammi. Mom said, "It's time to get in the car and get yourselves settled down."

Man, this was something…me, Olivia, Troy, Lorri, Lisa, Tammi, Melvin, and Mom sleeping in a car. I started hating Mom all over again. I left a place where there were people who cared about me. I even had my own bed. Now, we were on our way to Columbus in the middle of nowhere. How come she just didn't tell them again that she didn't want me? Everybody got a blanket except me. Troy was on the back seat, and I was on the floor. Same old shit, just like my past. They would make me sit on the floor of the car whenever we went somewhere. Mom said that I wasn't allowed to sit on her seats. I shook my head and lay my head down on a bag of clothes. I started getting mad because they didn't know who I was. "Adam?"

"Yes."

"Don't you fuckin' forget who brought your black ass in this world, and I'll take you out. Them white folks might been around you for sometime, but your ass is still mine. I wouldn't have to move if your ass was still in there. You want to know why?"

I didn't say nothing because she was drinking and still smoking cigs, and I knew how she used to be.

"They said I had to come and get you because some boy raped you. That's right, you been raped."

"No, I wasn't," I said with tears in my eyes. Nobody ever talked about that day. I wanted to go up there and beat her ass and then stick her with a knife. Everybody turned around and looked at me. I said, "What are y'all looking at?"

"Shut up, you fag," Mom snapped. At this time she'd hurt me bad, and tears were running down my face. "Let me tell your ass something right now, keep your mouth shut about that place. Don't touch my kids, and whatever I tell you to do, do it. Now lay your ass down. Fucking white people telling me if I want you back we have to move. I don't want you, they could have kept you. They were looking for me to come and get you. I thought when I didn't write or come see you they would have put you up for adoption, but your dumbass would come right back like your dumbass always did."

I was boiling mad at this point. I kept saying over and over in my mind when I get to Columbus, I'm running away. I'm not living this life with them again. I'm smarter now; I've been by myself since I was six years old. I'm eleven and a half now. I have money, I can get my own place, or live on the streets. It would be just like the center, everybody out for themselves. Some kids played around, snapping towels at people, turning hot water on people in the shower, gluing stuff to people. Some kids even shook a person down if you had something that they wanted. But only the big kids shook people down.

I played all kinds of tricks on people. Sometimes I got caught, sometimes I didn't. Now I wanted to play a trick on Mom and them. They'd been fucking mean to me ever since we'd left the center. Mom was drunk, and everybody else was asleep except her and I, just like in the past. She kept on talking about me and how I made her life hell. It was the same old story about my dad leaving her, about how she missed me, and now she had the real man back. I fell off to sleep, rolled up in a ball, scared. I feared that she might come and burn me with her cigarette or pour beer on me or hit me, whatever. In the center we learned that once we got to sleep, won't nothing bother you. That's what Ms. B said.

She always knew what to say to us. As I look back, I can't believe how some people really did care about me. See, I grew up in a small town with white people who didn't like blacks, and they had no problems calling you a nigga. My sisters, and I used to get into fights and throw things at people. Mom always told us about white people and how they would take some kids out to the woods and beat them. Then the sheriff would show up and bring them home. This was a warning for that meant the next time, he wouldn't be coming home. I used to think she was lying, but I'd heard boys talk about what their fathers did to some of their black workers. As the night went on every now and then, I would hear Mom say something, but I couldn't make it out because she was drunk. When morning broke, Mom woke me up first. "Adam." I heard her but I didn't move because the staff at the center didn't call me that. They called me Adam. She said in a strong, loud voice, "Adam. Hey, go get me a cup of coffee." I opened the trunk of the wagon, climbed out, and walked over to her. She gave me a dollar and looked at me. As we looked at each other Mom said, "Well I said where do I get it from? See, I know you're dumb because if I put or say to Adam, I need this he will get it. They fucked you up, and now I have to teach your dumbass all over again. Take your ass up there and put the money in the machine and get my damn coffee."

I walked by her, no longer scared, looking straight ahead. Mom smacked the shit out of my face as I walked by. "Don't roll your eyes at me," she said.

I wanted to say something to her, but the smack hurt too bad. Tears rolled down my cheeks, and I kept my mouth shut. I walked up the hill not looking back, hearing her voice say in a nice calm way, "Troy, Lorri, Lisa, y'all wake up and wash your face. We're getting ready to leave."

What the hell, I'm back in the same old game and this time...I won't lose. Everybody knew at the center if you did something to me, I would get you. Maybe not then but when I did, things would change your life forever. I learned while being locked away and from someone doing something to me, that I played to hurt. I hurt you hard because all I knew was pain. I put the money in the machine and looked at the buttons. They were funny words, but I could read them now. I was proud about some of the things I took from the center and some things I did not like. Sometimes staff acted like they liked you but before they left for the night, they would take almost all of your points away or not give you any at all. There were a lot of staff who didn't care for blacks; they always said mean things to me. And if you told on them, that would make it even harder on yourself. While you were there they would give the older kids special things if they somehow hit you a couple of times. I witnessed staff just turn their heads while this was being done. "Remember," they would say, "this is a center. Lay low until you get yourself together."

The center was surrounded by a twenty-foot steel-wired fence with razor-sharp blades on top. It panned out to be twenty-six feet of barbed-wired fence, a razor-fenced prison. Now I was back in another prison...I remembered that Mom liked her coffee black, straight black. She smoked Pall Mall red and drank Pepsi in the can. A short, and I mean short, smile came on my face. Now let's see what she says now. This coffee was hot. Wow, I thought, how can I carry this hot cup of coffee? Mom used to burn my hand on the stove burner. She would burn me if she heard that someone brought me home because I got caught stealing. "Stick your hand out and come here," she would say. I would cry, and that made her even angrier. She would grab me, and I would yell, "No Mom! I won't steal anymore."

My sister would come running out. "No, Mom, don't do that." But Mom would be drunk, and she'd tell them, "Shut the fuck up and go to bed." She used to beat me on the bottom of my feet so that I didn't sneak out the window at night. She'd taken my shoes and my clothes away. My older sister Lorri, who was seven years older than me, was the only person in that house who tried to help me. But she knew how Mom was. Troy was three years younger than me. Olivia was five years younger than me. Tammi was one year older than me. Lisa was six years older. I took my shirt off, holding the cup with my sleeves, and started walking down the hill. Lorri laughed. "You already getting your ass beat."

They were on their way to wash up at the rest-stop bathroom. I made it down the hill to Mom. "It's about time." Scared like hell, having to pee, I reached out slowly not to spill none on Mom. Hoping that she didn't hit me, I peed on myself. She grabbed it and asked, "Did you see Melvin up there?"

"No," I wanted to say. "Do you see Melvin up there, you dumbass?" That's what she liked to call me all the time, but then again, that was my mom. I walked to the back to get my stuff to wash up and brush my teeth just like I'd done for the past six years. I got a shirt, deodorant, pants, underwear, toothbrush, washcloth, socks, and T-shirt. I started running slowly up the hill to the bathroom. "Hey, where are you going?"

I looked around to see who said that. Mom said it again, "Where in the hell are you going?"

"To the bathroom to wash up."

"No, come here." I started walking down the hill. "Hurry up!" I moved faster.

"What is this shit?"

"My clothes and toothbrush."

"Yeah?" She snatched it from me and said, "Here, Troy, go get yourself together. Tell Tammi or Lorri to go to the boy's bathroom with you." Looking at me, Mom said, "Get your ass in the back."

I looked at my brother and the fact that he got my stuff, again. I looked at him with kindness in my eyes, but my thoughts were of a knife up to his throat.

"I said, get your ass in the back until we leave."

Now, for as long as I've known Mom, she didn't mess with Lisa for nothing. Lisa was mean like Mom, she didn't seem to like people much. Now, she was mean, and I didn't mess with her too much. She would beat you crazy.

Mom was dark with short hair. She wore glasses and would beat you up if you called her four eyes. I'd seen it. Lisa played sports in school and she was good. Lorri ran track and did art. Tammi was just plain smart. Troy was a king over everyone. Olivia was a little girl, real little. As for me, my family called me bad luck, thief, liar, and one who could not be trusted. I put my head down and walked to the back of this broken-down two-hundred-dollar wagon. Mom said, "Take Troy in there to change."

Under my breath, I called Mom a bad, bad name. And Troy, I'd deal with him later. I was sitting in the back when Olivia and Lorri came back to the wagon. Lorri asked, "Are you going to wash?" I looked around.

Mom said, "Leave him alone. Worry about yourself."

Lorri watched us when Mom was drunk, at the gambling joint or out with some drinking buddies. She was like our nice mom. She wouldn't hit me at all. I heard Mom yelling at Melvin, "We're lost."

Lorri and I looked. She said, "What?"

Melvin started to explain how to get there and then said, "We'll be there today. If you didn't have to get him, we would be there by now."

Lorri said to me, "You see, some things didn't change." Lorri had this thing about calling Mom *mom* when she was doing something wrong or bad. We all got back into the wagon and were on our way to Columbus. Everybody was laughing and talking around me. I was sitting on the backseat floor, thinking about Troy with my stuff on and was wondering what they were doing right now at the center. Probably eating, I thought. It was Thursday and I'd been gone for less than twenty-four hours, and I missed the place already. I wanted to go back. We stopped for some more food. Mom always ordered the food; she didn't ask what you wanted like the people at the center. Listening to them talk, I noticed that they were rude and very disrespectful. I had learned so much from the center, but I couldn't share it with them. They would just laugh at me, my sisters, and my brother. But if I kept it to myself and used it when I had to, I would be ahead of them. I saw how much they knew about me, which was nothing because they thought I'm that same person but I'm not.

We're laughing, playing "I spy." I started the game, but when you have a little brother, they want to say it all the time, and then you don't get a turn. He was making me mad. In the center we would have called him soft. Troy wouldn't last in there, he was spoiled, and he took my spot while I was gone. I was the oldest boy and then Troy and Olivia with me in jail. Olivia was next in line to be treated good.

"Oh, I know a game we can play, and everybody can play it. It's called y'all ready, hot hands."

"Ah, we know how to play that," Lorri and Tammi said.

Tim said, "I don't."

"Oh, I'll show you," I said. "Hold your palms down where your back hand is showing. Now I'm going to hit your hands. You have to pull them back before I can hit them. Okay?"

"Okay." I looked up front at Mom and Melvin, then at my sisters. They were looking at me and Troy. I didn't care. Mom was talking, and she had just opened some beer, so she wasn't drunk. Only thing she would say was for us to stop. Plus, I was eleven now, not four or five years old. "Okay, Troy, you ready?"

"Yes. Come on."

I nodded my head to see how fast he was. That's how I learned to beat the guys. It took me some time and painful hands to learn to be fast enough. I didn't hit him yet; I was setting all of them up. I shook my hand under his, he moved. Then I slowly tried to hit him and missed. I was trying to miss, but I also wanted us to learn to play together without them picking on me. After a while we had to lie down because Mom told us to.

"I can't get my drunk on with y'all up." So when she told us to lay our asses down, she and Melvin would talk, drink, fight, cuss, eat, and then sleep. "Hey, y'all. Hey, we're here." We all woke up looking forward to seeing what the city looked like. We'd seen enough small towns. Lorri asked, "Where are we going in Columbus?"

"Somewhere. We're going to go to a motel until we find a home," Melvin said.

We traveled the back way to Columbus from Cadiz. I was excited. We were going somewhere we'd never been before. This also meant that I was getting away for the first time in six years. I was glad, but Mom made my trip hell the whole time. Now, here in Columbus, we were moving on to new life and a fresh chance for me to show my family I had changed. One way they knew that I changed, I had muscles, and they weren't play muscles. I worked out, did chores, ran, and played. And I was eating three good meals a day. The girls at the center liked me, but they could only shy speak; that meant speaking hi, real quick, with their four fingers. Mom said, "We are in Columbus." I looked at everyone to see how happy they were. I didn't know why we were here and why we had a car full of clothes in plastic bags, but they were all smiling. So was I for now.

"Now, let's find a motel for the day." We came to Columbus fall of 1973, and it was a nice day. We ended up on Broad Street, two blocks down from the Y-kee-kee restaurant going east. We stayed there for a couple of months. I guess the real reason we actually came to Columbus was due to Melvin losing his job. When Mom and Melvin got into an accident, Mom was hurt and busted her ankle. And Melvin wired his mouth and some other things. Before we came to Columbus my mom and stepdad was in a bad car crash. Melvin had family in Columbus, and he used to come here when he was, what I would call somewhat dating Mom, even though he was married. Remember Melvin and my dad were best friends and they were both married. Well Melvin had a sister Jennie, who lived in Columbus, and she used to give Melvin information about jobs, houses for rent, where to look, etc. She knew who to call if you needed help getting food and clothes, and that was Franklin Country Children's Services. Now we're on the eastside of town looking for a place. Mom, Melvin, and I would leave out early to look for a home, while the rest of the family stayed at the motel. Almost everywhere we went they said no or something else. Mom was getting mad. We had two rooms next door to each other. I slept with Mom and Melvin, and the girls slept in the other room. We often played outside. The manager knew us real good, and so did the maid. Mom and Melvin would sit outside, drinking like always. At nighttime it was very pretty. All the lights to the buildings were lit up in different colors. Back home in Ohio, all of the lights were the same color, white. We liked nighttime because we would go to the end of the parking lot to look at the store lights. All of Broad Street would be lit. Well, as time went by, I was spending money here and there. Things were starting to get bad, and Mom was getting frustrated about finding a home. One day, Mom said, "I need you to go with Melvin."

I said, "Okay." I just wanted to get away from there. Melvin and I went to Kroger's. Melvin told me to stuff meat in my pants and pull my shirt down. I looked at him. "I don't steal."

"You did before and it ain't stealing. We just need something. We'll give them the money back later." Mom would say that they've got more than enough food. "Hurry and put that shit in there, so we can go." Mom wanted some smokes. I'm going over to get them for her. You do something to make people look at you while I do this.

What could I do? I thought. Maybe put my stuff back and then say, "Hey he's stealing." I smiled and said to myself, Mom would beat my butt. So I started dancing. People were looking at me and laughing. Some people gave me candy, some just smiled. Others walked by. I looked over at Melvin, and he gave me the nod with his head. As I continued to dance, I was trying to figure out how to get this stuff out the door without stealing it. I got it; I had money in my sneakers. I didn't tell anyone about it because they would have taken it from me. I've kept it in the bottom of my socks since I first got it. I knew this would have to work or I was dead. "Melvin, I have to poo."

"Hold it now. Let's go."

I stopped and said, "I can't."

"Okay. I'll be in the car." As he walked out the door, Melvin yelled, "Hurry the hell up!"

I smiled and walked back. I'd seen a worker and asked them where the bathroom was. They pointed, and I walked toward that way. Now let me tell you, if you haven't put frozen meat up against your stomach, I would say don't. I wanted to get it out and fast.

It felt like my stomach was frozen. I walked through the swing doors to the bathroom on my right. I took the meat out of my pants and placed it on the sink. I sat down, took my shoe off, and took out twenty dollars. I got up, picked the meat up, and walked out the door smiling because I didn't want to steal no meat, and especially not for them. I did what I'd seen everybody else do, I put the food on the counter and then handed over the money. I didn't see any kids buying or paying for things. Were kids allowed to buy stuff in Columbus? "Hi," she said with a smile. I smiled back and handed her the money, got the bag, and started walking fast. I was thinking about Melvin waiting in the car and how mad he would be at me and what he would tell Mom. "Hey kid, here's your change."

I turned and smiled, "Sorry."

"It's okay, put it in your pocket." With the money in my pocket, I went out of the store smiling, looking around for Melvin. "What the fuck you done now?"

"Nothing. When I walked in the store, there was twenty dollars on the floor, so I took the meat and bought it."

"Oh, Mom's going to get you."

"For what?"

"You'll see. I guess they did fuck you up." He didn't talk going back, and I was thinking and thinking fast. What was I going to say to Mom? I needed to just start talking and not tell on myself. Not even to my mom. Mom taught me that when I was growing up with her, but I added my own input after she left me in that awful place. I didn't play, I was out for me, and I was not trying to go to jail for anyone. I'd just returned home. We pulled up to the motel; we weren't far away. Everything that a person needed could be found on Broad Street, and we never went far from it. I guess Mom and Melvin's luck wasn't working too well because they had run off together to make a life for themselves, not us. And for damn sure not me. He hated me because of my dad. I was smart at the age of eleven. I knew how to clean a home, wash clothes, go to the store, and shop. I'd taught myself the art of persuasion, and I knew how to talk people into things. Melvin got out first, then me. I had a bag and Melvin had a box of smokes for Mom. The family came out smiling, asking, "What you got? Can I have some?"

"Stop. Give it back," I said as Tammi grabbed it from me. Troy smiled and stuck his tongue out at me, and I laughed at him. He didn't know that there was meat in the bag. Mom said, "Come here."

"Yes, ma'am."

"Melvin said you found some money. How much?"

I pulled all I had out of my pants. Mom smiled and said, "Next time do what I tell you. See those white folks got your mind all fucked up." Then she sent me outside with the kids and we played around the motel acting like we'd been knocking on people's doors and then running away. Mom cooked dinner. At night we would take a bath and then come outside and look at the lights before bed. I think we stayed there for some time before we found a house. One day Mom said, "We have to leave because money is running out."

I knew that I couldn't bear to see my mom cry. Even though she made me sleep on the floor and was trying to have me steal for the family again, I knew how to get stuff. When I was locked up, guys used to try me, but I never gave in. So I went into the bathroom and got some money out of my shoes. I counted it, $325. I set $300 aside and put the other money back in my shoes. I opened the door and came out and said, "Mom come here. I want to tell you something."

"A man dropped this money so I picked it up."

Mom looked at the money in my hand and smiled. She took it from me, asking and looking around, "Did anybody see you?"

I said no.

"Did you break into somebody's room?"

"No, ma'am."

She said, "Good." We went inside the girls' room. She said, "Here's twenty dollars for you."

I was happy she gave me money and hugged me. I felt something good then. It was a good night. We laughed, talked, and ate pizza. I was allowed to talk about me and the things that I had learned. We really didn't know each other, so I had a lot of questions. Some of my questions didn't nobody say anything, but we had fun that night because Mom said we were leaving there. I felt bad because I thought she was leaving because I gave her that money. Mom had said that a man had been walking around all day like he had lost something. I didn't say anything I just laughed. If she only knew where the money came from, but I couldn't tell her. Mom finally found a home; it was located on the east end of town. As we moved into this house on 18th and Franklin Avenue, we slept on the floor at nighttime because we didn't have any furniture or beds, and people were out fighting in the streets and tearing up stores. I later found out that we moved to Columbus after a little boy was shot by a laundry cleaner owner. Yes, and people were yelling, shooting, fighting, breaking store windows. Mom knew how to talk to people, so she could get what she wanted.

Our neighbor told my mom about this company who helped people like her. Getting free stuff was okay for a while. By us coming from a small town, we didn't know a lot of places like children's services and other organizations where people paid your bills and bought you food. It was almost like heaven. When my sisters went to Central High, Franklin, and Douglass School, that's when things changed. Mom started showing me some of the old things I used to do. By now, I was pretty wise. I'd been stealing bags of meat from various stores. I can't say what stores because owners might come back after all these years. I'm sorry, but I only took what my mom and family needed.

I was so good at what I was doing, that I moved up to bigger things like stealing brand-new cars. We would take them to Cleveland and sell them. I hooked up with some guys at Douglass Elementary, and they made me fight them all the time. I was short but fast, and we used to steal cars and teach ourselves how to drive. You would push your seat all the way up, put three to four phone books on the seat, wear a hat, and never look out your side window at nobody. Well, that went okay for a while until the amount of money we collected changed because we were kids. They would say, "Here's one thousand bucks."

"But you said three thousand dollars for every Cadillac."

Those were the only cars that we stole. I tried all kinds of tricks, sneaking onto car lots, stealing keys out of cars, even working for a car place on Saturdays. I would wash them and then hide the keys on the lot for my boys to come and get them. We never got caught stealing cars off the lot, but we had been chased by Columbus's finest. And everybody knew that you couldn't outrun a scared black kid. Things were so bad at home for me that every time we didn't have food, cigs, pop, whatever Mom would say. "Adam, go do this and don't take all day coming back." There were days when I would go after school to get things, or sometimes she would keep me home from school. Mom had even awakened me in the middle of the night. I took everything I could just to please my mom and to get outside with my friends. Even though these same friends would beat on me for fun and then say to me, "We're going shopping. Do you want to come?"

I would say yes, but I was always stealing for them or breaking into other people's homes. I had to climb through a window because I was smaller than the other boys. Mom and my sisters started hearing all kinds of stuff about me from their friends and neighbors. Now it was okay to steal for the family, but when Mom heard this, she called me and all my friends little niggers and told them my nickname. She told my friends that I wasn't coming out and for them not to come by. Mom was mean, and everybody knew it, but they liked her because my mom made jokes all the time and would tell our friends, "If you don't have five dollars, a pack of smokes, or Pepsi, don't come over my house." After sometime, my friends would come back.

Mom would say, "Don't leave off this porch." I'd wait until the music was loud or she was drunk, then I'd sneak off. I always got beat by Mom, and I still slept on the floor. I would come home late like 9:00 p.m. or 10:00 p.m. And sometimes not even at all. I was a big man on my street. People, my friends, they looked up to me. I was the only kid on my street with a .22. When we took our last car to Cleveland, Ohio, I stole my older sister's gun, and boy you should have seen the look on that man's face. My friends were like, "Put it down." "Where'd you get that?" "Don't shoot me!" They were all yelling. Now my friends had never been in trouble before they met me. They had good parents and nice homes. But not me, I couldn't bring my friends over. I would always meet them on the corner. Mom would be drunk, or she would say, "Your thieving friends can't come in here."

It didn't matter to me; I didn't have no bedroom anyway. I used to be jealous of my friends. They had kind moms, nice clothes, and their own bedrooms. They used to give me their old clothes, suits for holidays. Thank you, Gary, Bow, Ronnie W., Ronnie D., James T., and Arthur V.

"Give me what you owe me."

"What? What?"

"Two thousand dollars for every car we brought you and that three thousand dollars, and I'll be on my way."

Everyone was yelling at me until, finally, I pointed the gun at my friends. "Shut up," I said. I turned my attention back to the man.

"I don't have that much."

"So give me what you have."

He gave it to me, and we backed out of there. They talked shit all the way home, but we laughed hard because they thought they knew me. I was the man. When we went to school they told everybody about it. I had it made: money, friends, candy, and a gun.

You couldn't tell me nothing, not even my friends. I was a twelve-year-old with a gun, and I didn't care. I would say I found this or that and give it to Mom, just to get out of the house. I didn't take my clothes home or my money. I hid everything outside under the porch with my gun and then changed over my friend's house. I didn't want Mom to take it, and I didn't want my little brother wearing my new stuff. I was proud of myself. I was helping my family, and people were scared of me. My best hangout was Main Street, pimps, holes, dice, women, bars, and fast talking. Everyone always dressed up real clean. I was living in a world my mom didn't know about. I'd leave for school and stop off to break into somebody's home and steal money, meat, or whatever I thought was of value. The city was a nice place to live, but you had to remember that there were people out there willing to teach your child anything. Especially when it benefited them. I knew people who showed me how to look for money in homes, cars, and where guns would be hidden. These men paid good money to nine- to eleven-year-old boys. My friends would make me fight every day after school. Sometimes they would start before school. They used to bully me, talk about me, and even chase me home sometimes. I still hung around them anyways. I always had money or candy, and that would make them be nice to me. My friends would say that they were just playing with me, but I didn't think so. All the boys knew my mom was mean and that she beat on me.

One time my mom said she was going to teach me a lesson and had her boyfriend shave my head bald and put a yellow dress on me and walked me to school. Melvin then stood at the playground and watched me walk into school. I had tears coming down my face, my nose was runny, and all of my hair was gone. Here I was, this dark-skinned kid with a yellow dress on and some dirty, smelly, white tennis shoes. But those were my shoes. Mom always told me, "If you steal, you can steal your own clothes and shoes." As I walked to my class, kids were laughing at me, pointing their fingers at me. I didn't say nothing. I just sat there with my head down. Mr. Embry came over to me and said, "Come with me." I looked around the classroom and saw Gary, Lynn H., Bow, Anthony, and Mrs. Beverly laughing at me along with other people. I hated my mom so. When we went down to the office to see Ms. Vicken, Mr. Embry said, "It will be okay. She cares about kids." But I always got sent to her office for getting into trouble. I sat in the office and watched people as they stared, whispering back and forth. The door finally opened and she said, "Come in here, Adam." With her hand out she motioned for me to sit down. She asked me what happened, but then there was a knock at the door. "Come in." It was Mr. Embry. I liked him; he was nice to me, and he knew I was the poorest kid in his class and knew I got into trouble because my neighborhood friends made sure they came to school and told on me. But they made sure that they looked good. Mr. Embry helped me with my schoolwork, talked to me about getting into trouble, my mom, how things were at home. He even gave me lunch money and let me come to his home sometimes when school let out for the summer, to swim and play around. He lived in a place where people had nice, big homes and lived good. "Mr. Embry, can you tell me what's going on?" Ms. Vicken said.

"Well, Adam came in class dressed like this, crying. The class was laughing at him, and I walked over and told him to come with me. I brought Adam down to the office."

She looked at me and said, "Do you want to tell us why you're dressed in a dress?"

I said, "My mom made me wear the dress to school and shaved my hair."

"Is your mom home now?"

I said yes. Ms. Vicken and I went over to my house. She got out of the car and then me. I walked up the steps, opened the door, and went in. Mom asked, "Who the hell is that?"

I said, "Me."

She said, "What the F—you doing here?" I started to tell her, but she came in from the other room and saw Ms. V. "Who the hell are you?" And that's when all hell broke loose.

"Your son came to school like this, and it's not appropriate for Adam to be dressed like this," Ms. V. began.

"You don't tell me how to take care of my kids, and you don't come in my home telling me what to do." Then she went on about what I do in the neighborhood and how I'm a F—up. Only thing I know is that they yelled at each other. Mom finally said, "You can get your white ass out of my house." After that, Mom kept me in the house for a long time, and I didn't go to school for a while until children's services came. They told my mom that I'd better be in school, or she would be in trouble. That brought on another ass beating. If any of the kids asked me where I'd been, I would say that I was sick. But my friends knew the truth because they would ask my sisters or brother where I was. "He's in the house, he can't come out." So they knew Mom had beaten me too bad. And they knew when not to come over. Mom was hard and mean and didn't say nothing to white people. She was drinking more, and I was back to stealing from stores and from school. At recess, I would go back in the classrooms and go through pocketbooks, then run to the bathroom and put it in my shoes. Melvin took me to Kroger's to steal meat by putting it down our pants. That was so first grade. So the next time we went, I showed him something. I took some paper bags from the counter, looked on the floor for receipts, then got a cart. I got a lot of meat and put it in the cart. Then I moved over to an empty aisle, opened the bag, and hurried to put the meat in it. If somebody would come, I would act like I was looking or waiting on my mom. Then when they walked away, I finished what I was doing. If a store clerk came by, they would see the sales slip and just walk by me. When I got home, Mom was so happy. This made her boyfriend mad whenever Mom was happy with me. Every time Mom played cards or lost her money, or just had no money, I would go to Kroger's and grocery shop for my family. My mom liked to drink, so she would leave us at home and go to bars or bootleg joints. Sometimes they would hit her or push her out after she had spent all of her money and got drunk.

So I made sure that I broke into every bar and every bootleg joint because I didn't want her going there anymore. I would take all of their liquor and cigs, but they still opened up and Mom kept going. Whenever I heard around the house that my sisters would say they needed this or that, I would go out and get it. I would put it in the kitchen, so they would find it or put it in their rooms. Sometimes they wouldn't know who did it. Then sometimes they knew I did it. The people around me didn't know what I was doing, I hid it well. I would go to Lazarus for my outfits: one pair of Lee jeans, one pair of high-top Nikes, blue and white. A button-down shirt, one pair of socks, and some underwear. I did this every day until one morning while I was in class, the principal came in and said, "Adam, can I see you please?"

I looked at Mr. Embry and shrugged my shoulders. "I don't know."

"Please come with me."

I started to run out the school, but I didn't do nothing, so I was okay. I went into Ms. V's office and sat down. Now my principal had like a side door built onto her office, and these officers walked in. I looked at her like she had just killed her best friend. The officer asked me if I was Adam. "Yes."

"Please come with us."

"Is my mom okay," I asked? They didn't say nothing.

The principal asked, "What did he do?"

They said, "We can't say."

Let me tell you something, that moment changed my whole life forever.

Well, let me explain to you what actually went down. We were living on Franklin Avenue at this time; I was in the sixth grade. School was almost out for the summer, and I was glad. I couldn't wait. They left me in this waiting room; they said they would be back. Then somebody came in, asking me all sorts of questions about cars, some guys and body shops, breaking windows, taking money, and other things.

I said, "I don't know nothing."

They said, "We have fingerprints, blood, and videotapes of people going into these places and leaving."

I still said, "I didn't know nothing."

He sat back and said, "We're just waiting for your mom."

We waited and waited. Finally, Mom came and when she walked inside the room, a lady was with her. "What did you do?"

I said, "Nothing, I was in class and they came and got me."

The lady said she was from children's services and that she'd received a call from school about Adam being arrested.

Mom said, "That's not true. You see him, don't you?"

A man came in and introduced himself. He then started telling my mom about a group of kids stealing cars from body-shop dealerships. She looked over at me, but I said, "Not me."

Mom said, "Well if he said he didn't then what?"

The cop said, "We've been looking into this matter for some time now, and your son is one of the kids who is with this group. Your son will go home with you today, and we'll be sending you something in the mail."

I told my mom that I didn't do nothing and that they were lying on me. She just said, "You're not going nowhere, and don't have your hood friends ask me."

I knew that wouldn't last long; she needed cigs and pop. A couple of days went by and nothing happened. Mom said that I could sit on the porch but not to leave. Ten minutes later I was gone. I told my boys what happened and talked about the police coming to the school. They said all kinds of stories about me. My mom had called them, I killed somebody, and that I stole a bunch of candy. We lived down the street from the grocery store, and I would stop by and get my daily candy for me and my friends.

I said, "No, they said they would be in touch by mail. I'll be at school on Monday. Y'all see." We went to Blackburn Rec center, played basketball and ran around the track. We then went into the boxing room and messed around with B. Douglas and his dad. We ran up and down the halls yelling at Mr. Anderson and Ms. Homes.

It was fun playing and everybody knew me. They knew that I fought a lot and that I was no punk. As I would play with friends, my family didn't want me hanging out with them. They thought that I stole and fought too much when I was around them. Sometimes Olivia and Troy would come to the center and get me to tell me that some man was hitting Mom.

I would run down there to her house and beat them old men up. Well we got the letter in the mail for court. This would be my first time in trouble in Columbus. The judge put me on house arrest until my next court date, and Mom was mad. She looked at me with hatred in her eyes. I looked away without saying nothing. Mom didn't send me back to school. She said. "You won't go anyway."

At this point in my life, I was an eleven-year-old in the sixth grade, facing grand theft auto and breaking-and-entering charges. My sisters were mad at me, and I wasn't allowed outside. My friends came over one day and said that they were going to Kroger's for some perm kits. They said, "We know somebody who will give us $2.50 per box. Let's get 10 each."

I said, "I'll meet you at the corner of our street." Mom was drinking and listening to Gladys Knight. "I'm Leaving" was the song. I opened the back door real quiet, shut it, and ran fast to the corner. I got on one bike with my friend, riding on the handlebars. We were going down Main Street to Parsons, then to Kroger's. That was when the highway patrol station was on Main and Parsons. A car was coming down the same side of the road that we were on. It didn't stop. We tried to get the bike onto the sidewalk but not in time. My friend jumped off the bike, and I got hit head on. I broke my left leg in three different places. I went to a children's hospital to get fixed up. I had to wear a cast on my leg up to my butt. I was waiting on Mom to come, but when she got there, she was drunk and started talking loudly, yelling, "You were stealing. That's what you get."

We went home. My friends came over to see me. I asked Gary why he got me hit. He said, "I thought you were going to jump too, but instead you stayed on."

I said, "No, my foot got caught in the front wheel. Then the car hit me."

I still don't know to this day the color of the car, what size it was, or whether it was a man or a woman driver. It was the beginning of summer, the year was 1973, and already I was starting to believe my mom when she called me bad luck.

My leg was broken, and Mom kept me out of school. "It's almost out, you don't need to go. Y'all ain't doing nothing."

I had a court date coming soon. What else could go wrong now? My leg hurt, and I had forty stitches in my right hand. The day of court, Mom, Melvin, and I went downtown to the juvenile center. I was scared because I was going through this again, except I was older now. The people present were Montte Crockett, a lady from children's services named Merlin Jinnken a court lawyer and Ms. Bernice. Ms. Bernice was present because she was black, and Mom wouldn't talk to white people. She only spoke to them when she needed their help. I liked Ms. Bernice; she was nice and always gave me something. She would come by our house to see me and to check on Mom. Sometimes, Mom would hide me in the room and tell me not to say nothing and not to come out until she called me. Sometimes Ms. B would stop by unannounced. I would have cuts or black eyes, or I would walk with a limp from where Mom or Melvin had beaten the shit out of me with a shoe, belt, cords, boards, bricks, pots, and pans. When I didn't cry, Mom and Melvin would play tag team on me. After all the stuff I had been through, I stopped crying. It showed my weakness. My older sisters used to say, "Adam, just cry so they will stop." I wouldn't. After that they would kick me in my back, leg, or face and stomach. Then they would say, "Get over in that corner and face it. Don't turn around." I hated sitting like that because Mom would walk by and kick the shit out of me or punch me upside my head. Or Troy, my little spoiled brother, would mimic what he saw Mom do.

My sister would tell on him, but she would say, "So fuckin' what. That's what he need."

I learned how to watch TV without looking at it. I would have to sit there until the end of the night or until Mom got drunk. My sister Lorri would say, "She's asleep, go ahead and lay down." But if Mom said stay there, then that's what she meant because if I moved, I still had Melvin to deal with. I could listen to the TV and tell you what was on it.

I would listen to the shows and put my own imaginative spin to it. I didn't get to watch a lot of television because Mom said, "People who steal didn't watch TV."

I knew deep down that she knew she had made me like this, not me. When Ms. Bernice came to our house and saw me hurt, she would ask, "What happened, Adam?"

I would start to say, but then Mom would jump in, "He was out here fighting those damn kids, knowing he can't fight."

Ms. Bernice would ask, "Is that true?"

I would look at Mom, and she would look at me and I would say yes. I knew I could fight good, it was really Mom and Melvin beating me for no reason. But that would do nothing but get me beat more. Mom told me if I ever told on her that she would beat me and give me away to some jail.

"All parties for Adam Jones."

We got up to walk into the courtroom. I looked at Mom and Melvin, nothing. They didn't look at me. Ms. Bernice and the lawyer told my mom that I wouldn't get sent away because of my arm and leg. I smiled and limped my heavy left foot into the courtroom. The judge was getting on my mom about not knowing where I had been.

Mom told him, "I have other kids. I just can't pay attention to him." They started talking about the cars, sports cars, Cadillacs, windows being broken, doors knocked in, money missing, body shops being broken into with car-lot keys missing. I knew we had done some of those things but not all this. I was scared now. I wanted to tell on my friends. My lawyer asked, "Is this stuff true?"

I said no.

He said, "They have witnesses."

I looked at my mom. She was mad and it showed. Then Ms. Jenkins stood and said, "Adam's been missing school. He was put on house arrest a week later and got his leg broken by a car."

Mom said, "I didn't know he had gotten out."

Then Ms. Jenkins said, "The mom and stepdad drink. Mrs. Jones don't talk so Ms. Bernice does the visits."

Ms. Bernice said, "I've gone to the home and saw Adam with marks, cuts, black eyes, and dirty clothes. We have given Mrs. Jones clothes vouchers, shoes, beds and food."

Mom said, "And he gives it away or kids take his stuff."

Everybody was saying something about me, but I wasn't saying nothing. I wanted to say that they were all lying. I wanted to say that none of this was true, but I couldn't. It felt like my mouth was shut tight, my body couldn't move, and my hands were wet. Mom stood up and said, "These damn people are lying, and this boy don't listen to me."

The judge said, "Okay, before I say what I need to say is there anything else?"

Nobody said nothing. We sat in court at the table waiting for the judge to talk. The judge said, "Adam, do you have something to say?"

I looked around the table at everyone and then looked at the judge and shook my head no as I lowered my head. The judge said, "We are going to send Adam to Franklin Village for some tests and for the mom to take some parenting classes."

At that Mom got real mad and said, "I'm not doing those things because I didn't go out there and steal those things."

"Mrs. Jones, this is to help you and your family. You'll be able to get your son back home."

She said, "You keep him, I'm not." I looked at her and so did everyone else. She got up and said, "I'm done."

The judge replied, "We're not." She sat back down, looked at me and said with no words, just with movement of her lips: "I hate you."

I looked at the judge, then my lawyer, and tears started coming down my face. The judge asked the policeman to come to his desk. They said something and then the judge faced me. "We're going to keep Adam for some psyche test. This will also help the family."

Mom said out loud, "We don't need help."

The judge said, "Your son does. Will you work on him?"

"Adam," the judge began, "you go with my officer, and he'll take care of you."

I stood up and looked at Ms. Bernice and the lawyer, and said, "I thought I was going back home."

They both looked at me but said nothing. They just kept a straight face. Mom looked at something else in the courtroom. I couldn't believe my ears. It happened again. She didn't want me, and they lied to me again. The officer came over to me and said, "Would you please come with me?"

I tried to get up, but I had a hard time. My arm had forty stitches, and my leg was broken in three different places. I only had one crutch to walk with. The officer helped me walk through the back door by the desk. I didn't look back; I was hurt and hurt bad. I didn't trust Mom no more, and the lawyer didn't help, and the people from children's service didn't help. The door slammed shut.

The black cop looked at me and said, "Sorry this happened to you." We walked to the elevator and got on. "Do you like ice cream?" I nodded yes. "Would you like some?" I shook my head no. The policeman said, "I'm taking you to see a lady named Billy and she will take it from here."

The door opened, and there stood a lady with a bad right eye with a scar going down the front of her eye. It looked like somebody tried to cut her eye out. She spoke to the officer and then to me. I waved to her. In the background I heard a lot of people yelling and talking, but I couldn't see them. The officer said to Ms. Billy, "It's been a hard morning. Give him a break."

She looked at me and said, "I'll do just that."

As I walked down the hall with this lady guard, I heard people talking loud, some yelling behind doors, and some people twenty feet in front of me standing around this area with glass windows around it. These were kids. Big kids, little kids staring at us while I was walking in slowly with the guard. Some guys I knew and some I didn't. I nodded at some. As I stood there looking around, I saw doors made out of iron and little glass windows with numbers on them. It was about twenty doors. And what shocked me was this TV up in the air and five tables made out of metal with four metal seats hooked to them. And a small water fount and a door that said *restroom*. Some guys were sitting down, watching TV, some talking at the tables; all doors were shut. I was small, but people said I was built pretty good. So I know these guys like to fight because of the way they talked and carrying themselves just these few minutes I was there. I learned this from my early years with my mom. At this point of my life, I'm eleven years old, and I'm standing there with a sad look on my face, wondering what I have done. The guard asked me what do I go by.

I looked at him, dumbfounded. He said, "What they call you on the street?"

I said, "Adam."

"Okay, come in here, Adam, and have a seat. We have some paperwork to do."

I walked through the small doorway and sat down at this couch and small table. The lady guard said something to the other guard, then she walked off while some boys spoke to her, and some made smart comments. One guy I knew from the street walked by and said, "What's up?"

I needed to know how this guard was. He walked away.

The guard said, "I see you have some medical problems?"

I just looked at him like he was crazy. Ain't nothing wrong with me.

He went on to say, "This wing is the medical part, and by you having your arm wrapped with thirty-seven stitches and that cast on you, you can't be on the other floors."

I now started looking around to see who else had casts on and other things, but there was none, so that meant that some off these guys took pills, and some were crazy.

"Adam, Adam, did you hear? what I said?"

"No, sir, you'll be staying in room 16 until your next court date."

"Does that mean I can't come out my room until I go to court?"

"No, but will go over the rules after lunch. So let me show you to your room. You'll stay here until your name is called then you will come out shut your door and get in line."

I walked in sat on the bed and looked around the room and saw toilet with a sink over it and a bed with a sheet, pillow, blanket, and a 22. That's a little pocket Bible; that was what we used to call it. I heard them start calling people. I wanted to be ready when they called me. I didn't want anybody getting mad at me. So I waited by the door with my heavy cast on my leg and my wrapped armed and shut the door with my good arm. As I walked over to get in line, I looked at the clock and noticed that it was 12:05 p.m. There were two guys I saw from the street. We didn't hang out, but we knew each other from making money or playing basketball at the center. I nodded and got in line. We walked down this hall then made a left turn. I saw a brick wall with glass windows in it and some ladies with white clothes on putting food on the tables. As we walked through the door, the one guard was giving us silverware with napkins. Then we walked over to a table and sat down wait until everybody was seated, then we said a prayer then ate. We sat with the two guys I knew. One of them said, "We have twenty minutes to eat, then lunch is over, so we eat fast and talk when we get back."

"Man, what happen to you? Look like them cops got you."

Now I just laughed at him and what he said. Stuffing my mouth with food. Remember, I just came from court some hours ago, and my mom doesn't cook breakfast for me. So I was hungry. It started getting a little loud in there with us guys talking all at one time. The guard said, "Hey, let's keep it down."

They didn't wear uniforms, just plain clothes. The inmates wore these brown pants with a blue shirt that on the back of it said "Juvenile." You had to wear your own shoes. As I was eating and looking around I heard the other person at the table talking, but I was busy checking other people out. This was different, I didn't know what to expect. I just knew I had to watch my back. Everybody got up dumping their trace, then line up to get back people were looking at me saying what happen, or why you here. Who did that to you. I knew whatever I say, it would tell them.

When we got back to our block, one of the men said, "Bathroom break." That meant that one member of the staff would go to the bathroom and watch us guys, so there won't be fighting, and one would watch the rest of us. As I was here, my mind was everywhere else, what Mom was doing. And what my friends were saying about me now. I wasn't there, and school was going to be out for the summer. I didn't know if I passed to the seventh or not. For some rea-son this place wasn't like the place I just come from. Everything was metal or brick. No chairs, couches. Nothing but some metal seats. Some people were in their rooms with their doors shut, some watch-ing soaps and talking about what they would do if they were there.

"Adam," someone said.

I turned around, wondering who knew my name. It was that guy I sat with at lunch.

"Hey, come over here. We want to talk to you."

I limped over and sat down.

"Around here we try to stay with our own. They like these white boys more. So if you fight one, you'll get in big trouble. When do you go to court?"

I said, "I won't, then they put me here."

Then one person said, "You'll be here like me until you go to court. My mom and dad put me here, because I wasn't going to school and I took my dad's car."

The other boy said he set some trash cans on fire behind their house. The other boy started telling me why he was here, but I couldn't hear him because I was thinking about home and why my mom said she didn't want me back home.

She said these things whenever I got in trouble, and it always made me mad when she did that.

"Hey, what did you do?" I looked at them, and they said "You can tell us. We ain't going to say nothing."

As I was about to say what I did, I heard the staff member say my name. I was glad I didn't want to tell them my Mom didn't want me to come home. I got up and walked into the office. He said have a seat. I looked at him. He had big arms, a big chest, and he was white with a blond low-cut hair. The only time I've seen somebody that big was on TV.

"I'm going to talk to you about you stay here, the rules, your court date, visits, showers, eating time, laundry time. Medication time. Then when I'm done, let me know if you have any questions. Okay?"

"Okay."

"We don't know when your next date for court is, but the court is downstairs, and when they send up court dates to us we put them on the window, so the guys know when they have to go. We give everybody a toothbrush, toothpaste, sheet, blanket, pillow, shower shoes, laundry bag. One Bible. Everyone goes to the chapel on Sundays. Your parents can come and visit you. Two times a week. They can bring you socks, white T-shirts, underwear, one pair of tennis shoes, comic books, magazines, not dirty. Envelopes, stamps, paper pencils. Pictures of family and friends. If you go to your room, you have to shut your door and stay there at least forty-five minutes. The door is locked outside but open from the inside. Some guys take a nap, read, or just lay on their bed. No one can come in your room at any time. If guys want to trade, they have to ask staff first. No gambling. We know that guys do gambling, but we don't say too much unless it get out of hand. No fighting because we have to give a report to the judge when you go to court. No sex play, or you'll be in lockup. That's down the hall and around the corner. Some of these guys are up here because they take medication that we have to watch them, some steal them give them away. Some trade them, and some of these guys have to have them. You're up here because you got hurt before you came here, and we can't put you with the other boys. How old are you?

"Eleven."

"Do you have scares?"

"No!"

"Cuts?"

"No!"

"Do you take medication?"

"No!"

"Are you sick?"

"No!"

"Let me look at your hair for bugs. Now I'm going to give you this paper, and if you want to write your social work, court, home, pastor at the chapel, you have to bring it to me, to staff, and we will send it out. One bar soap, one white towel, one washcloth. Showers you can take whenever you wish. Everybody in their room at 10:00

p.m., lights out at 11:00 p.m. Everyone up at 6:00 a.m. Face washing, shoes, clothes before coming out of your room. Court starts at 9:00 a.m., so we wake them guys up first. No one can stand by that front door at no time unless we tell you to or for court. Do you have any questions for me?"

"No, I said."

"If I were you, watch what you say and who you hang around with because if you want to go home, you'll be good. The judge likes good reports from the staff, we can help."

"Can I go to my room?"

"Yes, but roll call is at 3:15 p.m. That's when we call your name. Why? We make our rounds to see if you're in your room. Okay?"

I was tired and my leg was starting to hurt. But they didn't give me pills at children's, and they said I broke my leg in two different places. I went into my room, closed the door, and stood there for a moment, looking at the three walls and my bed and toilet. Tears started coming down face, but I didn't know why. So I lay down on my blanket and fell off to sleep. When I woke, I got up and looked out my little window to see who was outside. Just a couple of guys. I opened the door to go out. And one of the staff said, "Get back to your room."

I looked at him real mean, and I heard the staff tell him, "He's new." I sat down on my bed and waited. If anybody looked out their window, you could see that the clock was ten minutes to three o'clock. I remember that court time was 3:15 p.m. That was why he yelled at me. I lay down until court time.

How long will I be here? I started thinking about the streets. What were they doing now? It was three o'clock, and we would be going to the store on our way home to steal some candy like we always did. Or Mom would keep me home to help her with the house. I didn't know when I was going to court or when I would see Mom and the family. But I did know that they were going to let me go. This was my first time in here DH. But I've been picked up for shoplifting, was taken home by police and waited for my mom to come and get me. Or someone would come over and tell my mom that I broke into their place or from them. But I've never been to court or stole. Locked up in Columbus, we have been here about two years already. I still remember when we first came here. Now, what can I say to these guys about me when they ask? I'll just tell them I'm here for stealing cars, that's part of the reason I'm here. I'm not telling anyone about my mom.

"Court time," I heard someone say; it sounded like a woman.

I jumped up and looked out the door window. It was a woman, that same one who brought me upstairs. She started knocking on doors. They said their names as she knocked.

"Adam," I said.

I heard keys at my door. I got scared. I didn't do nothing. Maybe I said my name wrong. It opened, and I could see her face: light skin with brown freckles and a long line going down her left eye. She smiled at me and said, "How you doing?"

"I'm okay."

"How is your leg?"

"It hurts a little."

"After court I'll see what I can do."

She turned and shut the door. I sat up and rubbed my face like it was going to be all right. I didn't want to thank about today or my family, so I started thinking about my boys and what we going to do when I get home. Nock come out is what I heard.

I came out, sat down, and looked at the TV. No one was at my table but me. A white boy came over said his name. I said mine. We was talking, and he was telling me what we did. Then the brothers came over and said, "Is this white shit bothering you??"

"No," I said.

He looked at them then walked away. He said, "They don't fuck with me. They know I'll beat them up, in front of the staff."

I looked at him like, *I'm not afraid of you. And for you to hit somebody in front of staff, that's bull—.*

"Remember, we got your back."

Now I was short, but I had muscles and heart. "Okay, but I can fight for myself."

They laughed at me and said, "Not looking like that," and walked away.

Another brother walked up and said, "I hate them. They think they are the boss of us, but you're not, the staff is. Hi, my name is Sam. Don't worry about them, they won't bother you because you're not white. They are scared of the white boys. How long you got here?"

"What do you mean?"

He said they kept giving me a court date and then kept changing it.

"What did you do?"

"I stole some cars."

"Are you the one? They was talking about you. I didn't know who they was talking about. Who was your boys over there? They said y'all was going to hang when you get out. I got in a fight with my sister and tried to cut here. My mom said I didn't have my medication, so that's why it happened. She said we have to see what the doc says. I been her seventy-two days already."

"Wow, that's long."

"Yeah, but not long as some other guys."

Then he started saying people's names and pointing at them, telling how long they been here and for what. He was half black, half white. His dad was white and his mom was black.

"They don't F with me because they know I'll kick them around this room. Adam, can you come here?"

I got up and he said, "Nice. Until you make her mad then she turns into a man." Then he laughed and walked away. As I walked away I said to myself, "These mothers are cray, I got to get out of here."

"I spoke with the nurse, and she will bring you something at med time about 4:00 p.m. Dinner at four thirty. I work first shift but I'm helping out. So stay out of trouble and away from some people. And just watch everything today. I'll give you a chore after dinner, something I know you can do. Visiting day is tomorrow, is your family coming?

I looked at her and said, "Me and my mom don't get along."

"What about your dad?"

"I never knew him."

"Hay they need to see you, your mom is just probably just mad at you. They don't know anything about you until the court sends the paperwork up on you for the social worker, then she talks with the staff about who you are. They will try to help you—the guys. If you follow the rules, you'll do fine. Don't steal, fight, or put your hands on anybody. You should go home on your next court date."

I smiled and walked away. Will time came the guy's start liking me some was afraid of me and some didn't like me because I was a mouth talker. Plus the staff liked me. Sometimes I was going to court, but my mom never showed, so they said, "We'll send her another court time."

Every time I came back, I would look sad and mad, so guys wouldn't say nothing because other guys would say and then walk over to me and say sorry. Do say no. Because I didn't know if my mom had a phone or not. They would say to me, "Is there anything you want of mine before I give it away?"

If someone went home, they were happy and would give all their stuff away. And their good stuff along with their number to a good friend. I ended up being one. By now everyone knew that my mom left me in here and what I was here for. Stealing cars worth up to fifty thousand dollars, breaking and entering, four counts of trespassing, damages, stealing, skipping school. Everybody knew that if you said something out of the way to me I'd go off. I had to be sent to my room a lot for getting into trouble. Bullying people, gambling, taking things. I stole a cigarette lighter from female staff. Lying to staff. But people still felt sorry for me because I had a broken leg. But I'm about to get my cast off soon. My date was coming up. I had thirty more days to go. I was looking forward to it. I've been here for some time now, and the only person I was seeing was my social worker staff. I started getting to know the staff. They would say to me, "If you don't bother people, I'll bring you this book, food, candy."

Everybody had visitors except me. Money on their books to go to the store. I would have to ask for something or play cards for it, manipulate people. At this point I didn't care. I was friends with white people, black, it didn't matter. Mom would come see me. Guys would talk about their families. Sometimes I would get mad because I couldn't talk about mine. Today the day I'm going back to court without a cast. I sat in the chair. I was next to go in. I walked into the courtroom looking around for Mom. Nothing, just some people sitting at the table. The officer in the courtroom showed me to the front. A lady looked at me and said, "Hello, my name is Ms. Charolette and I'm from FCCS. I spoke with your mom, and she said she'd be here. I smiled and said okay.

"Is everybody here?"

"No, Judge, still waiting for Adam's mom, She said she'd be here today."

"I'll give her ten minutes more."

"Yes, sir."

The man came over to me and said, "You have a good judge, but you done a lot of bad things. The good thing is, you've been locked up about four and a half months. So that is a good thing. When your mom shows, we will try to send you home. Maybe some home visit with probations."

I smiled and said ok. Then he went on to say that the judge would have to decide something on this case. "You already had other dates."

He sat down at the table, and the other women came over, saying, "How you doing?"

I nodded okay.

"Have you seen your mom or family while you were here?"

"No."

"A letter?"

"No."

Now she was making me mad, asking me this stuff.

"Okay, let's get started. All people rise."

I stood and looked around the room. No Mom. I lowered my head, and I felt a hand on my shoulder. I looked up. It was that white lady from FCCS, smiling.

"It's okay, she'll be here."

We sat down.

"Adam Jones, four counts of grand theft auto, four counts of breaking and entering, property damages. Skipping school. Does Adam Jones have anything else?"

"Yes, Judge. Adam was sent away at the age of six years old for stealing people's mail and breaking in homes. He was sent to a home center for youth until he turns twenty-one or until his mom moves out the county. Adam moved. They came to Columbus, that's when FCCS came about." She stood and thanked the judge. She started talking about when they first got involved with us, how my mom didn't have no food or a place to stay. She went on to say that we were living out of motels and our car. She also went on telling how if they needed to come over to see her, my mom would be drunk and wouldn't let her in. Or would call them names. If we spoke with her about Adam missing school, she would say, "He ain't here" or "Why don't you go find him?" She also went on to say, "Before this matter, Adam's mom said he was on his way to steal. That's how Adam broke his left leg while being in the DH. His cast was removed off his leg a few weeks ago.

"Is this all?"

"Yes, your honor."

"Do he have someone here to help him?"

"Yes, Judge, a lawyer from the legal system Adam has been locked up about eighty days, Judge, and he had been doing well here. Some small spats but no harm to others."

"Are the parents here for Adam Jones."

No one said anything. Everyone looked around but no sing of Mom. Then the judge said, "Okay, here we go then."

It got quiet; he was writing something down.

"Where's your mom?" the lawyer asked. I looked at him and shrugged my shoulder. He said, "It'll be okay."

"Adam, do you have anything to say?"

"No," I said.

"Okay, please stand." We all stood up. My lawyer the repeat lady from the D.H. Center and the FCCS lady. All I could think about was where was Mom and why hasn't she arrived. Questions rolled off my mind, but I had no answer for her. Just Mom doing what she knew best. I heard the judge talking, but I was so much into what I was thinking. I didn't hear him.

"Do you understand what I just said to you, Adam?"

I was mad, so I said, "No, Judge, I didn't hear you."

That was when he asked, "Do you have trouble hearing, or you don't understand?"

"I don't understand."

The judge just looked at me and said, "Your lawyer will explain it to you."

They showed me out the court door to this other room. "Have a seat, your lawyer will be in soon."

I sat there with tears coming down my face. I tried to stop the tears, but it seemed like my face was running water; it wouldn't stop. It just kept coming down. The door opened. I started wiping my eyes, so the lawyer wouldn't see them. "Adam," he said, "I'm sorry, your mom wasn't here, maybe things would have been different. Well, let me explain. What happened just now is the judge said you will be placed in Franklin Village. You will seek one-on-one counseling. About your stealing, your anger, and possibly being put with another family."

I looked at him like he was about to get beat up really bad. I yelled real loud, "You lied to me! You said I was going home! I been here long enough!"

"Adam, please sit. I think the judge didn't want to send you back home to your mom because she didn't show. Well, maybe she had something to do or something happened. Mrs. Bience said she talked with your mom some days ago and let her know you was coming to court today?"

I said, "How long do I have to stay there?"

"We don't know. It will be up to them at Franklin Village."

"Why can't I go home? I've already been away from my family for four and a half months now."

He looked at me and I at him; he was a thin white man with glasses on. Blond hair and a suit that was too small for him.

"You hate black kids, don't you?"

"No, Adam, I don't hate black kids."

"Well, how come you didn't talk for me?"

"Adam, I did what I could. I think the judge had his mind made up. Already your mom didn't show for none of your court dates. So he felt she didn't care about you."

"Hey, my mom cared about me," I said in a low, dark voice.

He stood and said, "I'm really sorry." Then he said, "If you need me, here's my card. Call me."

While he was handing me his business card, I sat there with my hands crossed, looking away from him. He laid it down on the table and knocked on the door to be open. The guy stuck his head in and said, "I'll be back soon."

I liked him. I've been here for some time now, so I got to know a lot of the staff that worked there. When I got into fights, they were always bigger than me, but that didn't mean anything to me. Because I learned how to fight, and when I fought, I used whatever I saw that I could pick up and use in the fight. I had a plan when I fought. If you talked while we were supposed to be punching, I was going to hit you and keep on hitting you.

Kids, moms, and dads would come and visit on Sundays. I would get up, brush my hair, put my clothes on, and wait until visiting hours were over, hoping and praying for Mom to come. At 4:00 p.m., it would be mail call. I would be first. Maybe Mom wrote me to tell me she was coming to get me out of here like all the other white kids, or maybe my sisters wrote me and sent me money, clothes, or shoes. The staff would say to me while rubbing my head, "Not today, Adam, maybe tomorrow."

I would say, "Are you sure? Their ain't no mail."

"Yes, I'm sure."

Sometimes the guys would try to be nice to me and say, "Adam, come look at my picture" or "When I go to the store, I'll get you something." Or "Hey, do you want *this or that*?" Sometimes I would say yes. And other times if I was thinking about my mom, I would get mad and say, "I don't want nothing from you white people."

Now I don't know what to do because I told everybody this morning I'm going home. The staff was happy for me, and all the guys were happy for me. Now I have to go back upstairs and face everybody. And to make matters bad, they will move me today off the medical floor because my cast is off.

The door opened, and the big light-skinned man said, "Come on, son, it's time."

I walked out the door with my head down. The man put his hand on my shoulder and said, "Things will start looking better for you."

I looked up at him with my runny nose and tears in my eyes. He smiled, and we walked to the elevator. We walked in, the door shut, and the man said, "I don't do this for people, but I heard what the judge said to you. And where you're going is better than this place. If you want me to, I'll stop or call your mom for you and see what happens."

I looked at him and didn't say nothing. He looked at me and said, "Are you okay with that?"

I opened my mouth to say something, but nothing came out. I tried again.

"I don't know my phone number, and I don't know my address."

He said, "Don't worry, when they give me your file, I'll look and see, okay?"

"Okay."

The elevator stopped; the door opened. The staff said, "Hi, Adam. I hope things went well."

I looked and walked over to the wall to be patted down. Whenever you left you had to be checked again. People brought money back from court, also drugs, weapons. They even tried to run while they were in court or spit on people, fight, but all that would do for you is send you to lockup and get a case against you.

The man said, "I'll be back this afternoon with Adam's file," then winked at me.

"Did your mom come?" he said, trying to make small talk while he was doing his job checking me in.

"No!"

"How sad. What about your other family members?"

"No, sir. Okay. It's almost time for lunch, so just relax until then.

All the guys came over to me, and some didn't.

"Adam, my man, when are you getting out? Another guy said can I have your stuff."

Then my friends came over. They knew something was wrong with me, because I wasn't smiling, and everybody you see with a smile on their face you knew he was going home. But my face, there was no hope, no laughter. My eyes were red. They said, "Move back, let him breath, he'll talk later."

That was when the staff came out and said, "Adam, you okay?"

I turned around and looked over my shoulder. "Yes, sir."

Everybody got ready for lunch. That meant wash your hands and fix your clothes. Today was Thursday, and lunch on Thursday meant cheeseburgers, fries, juice, or milk. I told the staff I didn't feel like eating.

He said, "What's wrong, you sick?"

"No, sir."

"Somebody bothering big bad Adam?"

I smiled and said, "No, sir."

He always said something about my name. He liked kids, and he always told me it was hard to frown when you have a great smile. The other staff came over to us and said, "We're ready for lunch." He said, "You go ahead, we'll be right down."

We went into the office. He sat down and said, "Please sit."

I did sit.

"I heard a little about you today and court. I know since you've been here no one has wrote you or seen you. I wish I could take you to my home where there is love, not saying your family don't, but I've been reading your case since you been here. I want you to hold your head up and walk like you're proud of who you are. Sometimes parents say and do things they're not proud of later in life. Someday you'll look back on this day when things don't go your way. You have to keep looking for something better. Now we're going to help you get your mind back, but you have to promise me you'll do the best you can for you and me. Now you have to come to lunch because the cook made you something. And I wasn't going to tell you, but when I heard what happened, I knew I had to do something for you."

I looked at him happy but sad at the same time. I just wanted to see my mom; I haven't seen here in some time now. He went on to say, "Some guys will tease you, then maybe not. But don't you get yourself in trouble for them, just come let us know. Don't hall off and hit them out of anger. I've never been put in look-up. But it sounds like he will do it this time. Okay?"

"Okay."

As we walked out of the office I said to him, do you think she'll come see me this Sunday?"

"Yes, Adam. Now that she knows you have to leave here, you'll see her."

I smiled and said I hope so.

"You ready to eat?"

"Not really, but I'll go."

"This is your favorite lunch, cheeseburgers and fries"

"I know, but not today they're not."

He put his hand on my shoulder. "Come, let's eat."

As we walked down the hall, I saw some staff I said hi, and they would say, "Good afternoon, Adam."

When we walked into the dining area, everybody was eating, and some said, "Hey, Adam, come sit with me."

I walked through the line, and the older cook with white hair and a small body than mine said, "How is Adam today?"

"Fine, I guess."

"Well, I'm not giving you no food until I see that pretty smile of yours."

I gave her that smile, and she said, "There, that's Adam's smile I know."

I sat down and looked at everyone eating, not wanting to be here. I just felt like dying and not waking up anymore. Who would care? Not my mom or my dad or sister's brother. I looked at the staff, and they were looking at me. Pointing at my tray with their lips, saying, *Eat, it's okay.*

I looked down at my food; it was still lot and time was passing by. If I started eating now then we would have to stop eating and go. I was hungry but not wanting to eat. I pick up my burger and started eating. I had my head down, biting my burger. Then I heard people clapping. I looked up, and they were looking at me. The two cooks came out carrying a small cake. As I looked, I was saying to myself, *It's not my birthday, so what's going on?* The cook said, "I heard you were having a bad day, so we thought a cake would have made you feel better about yourself. Adam, we made your favorite cake chocolate on chocolate. Please cut the first piece, please."

I looked at her and said, "No, thank you."

She said, "If you don't, I'll cry right here," with a half-smile on her face I said okay. And I cut the cake; everybody clapped and said, "Okay, Adam. Today is your birthday. How old are you?"

"I'm eleven."

This was the first time they did this for me. I've been here four months, and the only thing they would do for someone is give extra food, snacks at bedtime. I know why this was happening; it was because the social worker kept asking me how I felt with no visiting time from my family, and I always asked the staff a question.

"How do you feel?" I would say as I ate my cake while thinking about how long I would be there. I was so damn mad at Mom. I've been here with no mail, no visits, just like back home in Cadiz, same old stuff.

"Adam? Adam, are you okay?" Someone was shaking my shoulder. I snapped out of daydreaming and yelled at him, saying, "What do you want?" in a loud voice.

He said, "My bad, man, staff was calling your name and you looked like something was wrong with you inside. Adam, come here please."

I got up and hit my boy on the arm. He looked at me and smiled. I nodded my head back with my slow, limping walk. We knew that we were cool because that was our sign, a hit on the arm. We had everybody else scared of us. He started to say something, then I cut him off by saying, "Man, he kicked my chair. I didn't mean to be loud."

"It's okay, not that I've just talked to the nurse, and she said we don't have to move you now because you just got your cast off and you're going to need some more time with that leg."

I smiled and said, "Thanks, Mr. Jones."

He was nice and he worked with the older kids in the DH. But he would come down and get us and take us upstairs to see the big boys and hear their stories about what they had done. Mr. Jones always tried to scare us or tell us about us, and some didn't and most of the staff did good things for us, and some did bad things. But the longer you're there the more you learn, some things you don't say or talk about what had happened inside those places.

"Now, Adam, I don't want you fighting, stealing, lying, or making people buy you stuff from the store."

As we were outside the lunchroom listening to Mr. Jones talk about me, I was thinking, shouldn't he be upstairs?

"Okay, Adam, can you keep yourself together until they let you know when you're leaving?"

"Yes, Mr. Jones," I said with a short smile on my face. Mr. Jones went on to say that he thought it would be better for me to stay on the medical ward because when you're not hurt or sick, you're with your age group. I wouldn't be able to keep up with the guys upstairs. I walked back into the lunchroom. The staff was having people throw their stuff away. My boys asked me what happened, I said nothing. They laughed at me and gave each other high fives. I looked.

They said, "Mr. Jones was either telling you about yourself or telling you what he should be telling his kids."

I said, "Right, right."

The cook said to me as I was putting my tray up, "Can I get you something?"

I said no.

"So I and Mr. Jones made you a cake."

I said thank you and smiled. She was about twenty-four or twenty-six years old. She caught me crying before, and we had a small talk, and staff loved to share kids' business. At their lunchtime. So everybody who worked there knew what you were in for. Everybody was a social worker, even me, laugh—laugh.

Tammy would always say, "You're my little brother, but you can be bad at times."

I would just look at her and smile. At her honey-brown sugar skin and just smile at her. Listening to my boys say, "Adam got a girlfriend" or "Man, she really like you."

They always cracked on me because I was short with dark brown skin, curly hair, with long eyelashes. They would call me Adam B. Scadeddie, do you need a chair to get that? Or your arms are too short to box with God. But they never said anything about my family or personal stuff. They knew I would go off. I beat some boys up. But we were good friends. Two of them I knew from my hood and the other guy I met here. And we looked out for each other. They even asked me if I wanted their families to visit me or their sisters. I would say thank you but no thank you. They would shake their head and say, "I don't know how you can do that."

I just said, "You can't get mad over somebody else and walk away before," a tear came to my eye. As we walked down the hall, some guys would ask, "Why did Adam get a cake for his birthday?" They were smiling and hating on me, another person said, because he is short. Then I said, "Because I'm Adam Jones."

Everybody started laughing at me. It was time to go back, take court, and chill for a couple of hours then get ready for court time. Normally my boys and I would go back and play spades or tonk. For snacks, shirts, shoes, whatever.

It was okay. I won a lot because they didn't play like I did. My mom and big sisters showed me how to play. And I took every game for real. They would play around; that was because they had visits, money on their books, and family. Only thing I had was me, and I never played around, not unless I was cheating you or you had something I wanted. But today was different. I didn't really want to play today. I felt like crying and staying in my room. Things didn't go my way, so I was going to tell my boys what was up. The door opened, and we started walking in when all you can here turn to the young and restless. We loved to see the women on the show. But today I didn't. Normally I would crack a joke on them, but not today.

"Adam, you ready?"

"Not today."

"Ah, come on, I won't beat you too bad."

I smiled and said, "You're right because I'm going to my room for a while. I'll see you guys after court. Okay?"

"Okay, Big Adam."

Then all the guys started laughing loud. I just walked away. I didn't know what to do. My eyes were sleepy, but I wasn't. My heart hurt real bad. I haven't much seen my mom or sisters in some time. We were allowed to make phone calls on Sundays after chores. But I didn't have my family's numbers, so I would seal my phone time sometimes or stay away from people when I'm upset, thinking about my family. Guys would see me upset and not ask. Care about nothing, not even myself. I walked over to the table and said, "Just one game. Because I'm not in the mood."

"What's wrong, you sick?" the white boy said.

"No, I'm just tired of being here."

Everybody started laughing. I never had to put anything in the pot because I was so good; everybody wanted me to play cards with them. I would always win, most of the time I cheated like hell. I would lie and bully guys out of their game. There was this one guy in DH. everybody talked about. It was something like a myth. Guards would talk about this boy who liked little boys, and he had a burned face.

But we would laugh and say what we would say: we'll see someday. I wouldn't say nothing, just look at them. I was scared, but I also knew ain't nobody going to hurt me anymore. I don't care who it is. When we went to bed, we would make some kind of noise so the guards would get up and down. Some guards would let you stay out until your shift was over. Some would ask for favors. They would ask me sometimes, but I would say no. I didn't want guys calling me a snitch. I work hard on my chores, and staff liked me. But everybody know the staff white guy's and have sex with them men and women. The morning came; it was 5:00 a.m. You get up, wash your face and hands, put your clothes on, then come out and sit down until count. For some reason I was the first one out my room. Guys and staff knew how I felt about my family not coming to see me. *Knock, knock* then the door opened.

"Adam, you coming out?"

"No, not right now."

He said okay and shut the door. I lay there, thinking to myself, Okay, you're about to ship out. You need to make a name for yourself."

I had a cast on my right leg, broke it in three different places. And I'm short. I've been there about seven months, and usually people, inmates, would be shipped out, but they didn't really know where to ship me. And I just heard that some guys leave to Moehkeen, Franklin Village, Buckeye Boy's ranch. Or other places. Staff would tell you when you were going to get shipped out day and month. That made it easy for guys because if you were a bad boy, that meant you could get into fights before you rode out. Or some guys would wait until one day before they left and beat guys up or get beat up. I knew my time was coming. They were moving me out, and was not going to see my family again just like before. I wiped my eyes, sat up on the side of my bed, and looked at the walls in my cell. And I said to myself, "Adam, you're the man now, so act like it."

That was what my mom used to say to me. I opened the door.

"Hey, I want Adam to be my partner." They were playing spades for Snickers and pop. That was my game. I would pass cards under the table to win or get real mad and say I quit just to get my way. These guys were soft and had families who cared. I didn't. I walked out, said good morning, and walked to the showers with my towel.

"Adam," came a voice from the office. "They're going to move you sometime today."

I looked at him and said, "I thought I was going to stay here in the medical ward until I leave."

"I don't know why they want to move you. Get a shower and we'll talk."

I turned and walked away, mad, and with tears in my eyes. I knew all the staff, the guys, and everybody knew me. Some guys didn't like me because I didn't like white people, so I picked on them the most. I couldn't believe they were going to move me. Court time came. We lined up. My boy said, "I've seen the paperwork. You and four other guys are being moved today."

Now normally my dude would tell all the news about people, but today it seemed like he was holding back. "Dude, you know where I'm moving to?"

He looked at me and said, "Not now. Wait until first shift comes on."

First shift was his thing; he liked one of the guards, and I thank she liked him. We never did chores on first shift while she worked and never had to be put in his room for lunch count and second shift. I thought he was telling on people, so I watched him close and what I said. But he was cool. He was about 5'6", white, about 140 pounds, brown skin with a perm. Some guys said if he didn't like you, he would tell on you. Chowtime, line up. Adam, I hear they're moving you."

"Yes, that's what I heard too. And smiled at him.

"Are you scared?"

"Of what?"

"Moving to another floor with older kids I don't know, we'll see what you're talking about."

We went back and lined up for court. Then we went to our rooms until staff started cell cleanup and duties, and the people ready for court. We came out of our room. My boy walked over to me and said, "Sit down, look at this."

I looked over my shoulder to see where staff was in the office doing paperwork, handing out chores. I looked down. I couldn't believe my eyes; it was Marjay. I looked at him, and I didn't smoke that shit. He said, "Neither do I, but staff bring it in for me. And I sell it to the white boys for money, snacks, whatever, man. I'm not going home their moving me they will find it. No, they won't. Now my boy has been in and out of DH, so he was smart and a lot of staff knew him by name and like him. I trust my boy, but he could get into trouble if you don't watch out for yourself."

"No, I'm cool."

"What?"

"Man, I want to go home."

"Adam, you're not going home and you know that."

I looked at my dude and didn't say nothing, looking up at the TV and said, "You have to handle you own problems. He started to get up and looked at me and said, "You scared of these white boys? Maybe they should move you."

I couldn't believe he said this to me, and I had been cool for two and a half months. We met in here. I jumped up on the table and said, "Scared? You think I'm scared of these white boys?"

He looked at me and smiled while walking toward me. "Okay now, we're getting somewhere. Adam, get off the table now."

I looked at staff and then back at my dude. I looked at him and said, Adam Jones ain't scared of nobody, even these guards. The staff looked back at me because I said it loud enough for them to here. Guys said, "Oh wow." I looked up at the staff and said we were talking about something not about staff. If you plot something or threaten staff, you would be put in the hole. That mean another floor where bad kids go and you're locked in your room. That wing for fighters, people who steal from staff or each other.

"Man, are you okay?"

"Yes, but let's stop talking in line before we have to clean."

No talking. I sat down at the dinner table for breakfast. My boy said to me, "Now would be a good time to get that white boy back who told on you."

I looked at him and said, "Yes it would, but you know he ain't going to do nothing but tell on me. Then I'm in trouble.

"Maybe, but you're moving."

I looked at the white boy and then back at him. Took a bite of my oatmeal.

"you just want me to handle that mess you got yourself into with him."

My boy was tall and skinny. But he couldn't fight for nothing. He would talk all this stuff to you then say, "I'm trying to get out, you're not going to keep me here."

"Adam, I thought we were boys and stick together. I did have a problem with the white boy before, but now you see he gives me stuff from his visit: T-shirts, socks. Me and him are ok. I'll pay you what can you give me. You'll see."

I looked over one more time at the white boy. He looked and smiled. I nodded my head at him.

"What you say, Big Adam?"

I kicked him in the face real hard, then jumped on him and started punching him. Yelling at him. "Scared? Adam Jones ain't scared of nobody."

Only thing I heard was "Stop punching him!" and staff grabbing me. As I was yelling, "Get off me," I saw all the other guys looking at me. Staff took me into the office while the other staff handled the other guy.

"Adam, what's wrong?"

I looked at him, not saying anything.

"Is it about you being moved? Are the guys teasing you."

I looked away. "If you are in solitary for a couple of days, okay," I said and sat looking out the office window, not caring about what was going to happen. I felt good my first fight in jail and thinking about what have happened to me last time I was locked up. So I made sure I get this dude good, so everyone will see I'm not to be f— with. As I was daydreaming I heard the guard say, "We are going to let the nurse see you, and then we will move you upstairs."

I looked at him and said, "I'm not scared of those guys up there.

Staff looked at me and said, "I know you're not, plus some of my friends work up there, they'll watch out for you."

Now people were tripping off me because I was real little and fought a lot and had a lot of mouth. People would say, "Go sit down, little boy, or punch me in the arm or stomach." Or me in the arm or stomach. My punches were just as hard as the older, taller kids. The guard said, "Now go get you things before the nurse gets here."

That was when the phone rang.

"Hello?"

He said, "Hi. You okay? Will see you soon."

That was the nurse. "It seemed that Adam broke his nose, and they think they want to charge him for it. So we'll take him down to the nurse, then we have to put Adam in lockup until a report is made and statements taken. Then the shift supervisor will make a decision."

I looked up at them. "How long will I be locked up?"

"We don't know. The boys' mom has to be called, and you know know about your parents. So I'm sorry you got yourself in this mess.

"Come on, let's see the nurse," I said out loud. He deserved it; some people are to be left alone.

"Adam, I know you're a good kid. You been here for six months now, and nobody ever stayed in juvenile this long, but you're a special case. So we are going to help you out."

"I looked at him and said, "They going to lock me in a room."

"No, we have a floor where kids go to calm down, or those who had been fighting. Your door is locked at nighttime but will be okay."

I was walking now down the hall to the nurse's station.

"Hello, Adam," she said. She always smelled good, and she was pretty, with a nice body and long shiny hair, with blue eyes. Her skin was white as milk. Then I looked her in the eyes and smiled at her and said, "Hello to you."

"Let's take a look at you." She went on to say, "I saw the other guy. You two must have really been mad at each other."

I looked at her and said yes. But I was thinking the whole time that she was trying to get me to talk, so they could tell on me, then I was going to tell but I decided to deal with him myself. AdamLHow did this happen? I looked at her and said, "I'm not hurt, and I'm not saying nothing until he says what he has to say."

"Who are you talking about?"

"That white boy, Tony."

She said, "He already told us what happened. Now we want to hear it from you."

I looked at her and said, "Ms. Brown, I don't have nothing to say."

"That's your choice, but if you don't talk, how can we help you?"

I looked at them with real mean eyes. "You can't."

Ms. Brown leaned over to me and said, "I know you're scared, but you have to tell us what happened."

I looked at her with pale white eyes with a black dot in the middle of the white. I said, "You mean to tell me that if I say what happened, you will believe me?"

Then she said, "Our staff will decide who is telling the truth, then we can move from there."

I said, "Okay, but I'm telling the truth."

She said, "I know you are, so what happened?"

I started talking, and then something happened. I didn't know what, but some women came in and spoke to Ms. Brown. She looked at me and then said, "Would everybody please step out?"

I got up, started toward the door, and then I heard "Please stop, Adam. I want to talk with you."

I stopped and hesitated before I turned around slowly, looking at her, thinking about what happened. Did he get really hurt?

"We just got in touch with your mother and explained what's going with your case and you."

I looked at Ms. Brown with a smile on my face, thinking to myself I haven't seen Mom in so long. She was coming to get me. Now I can go home. As I stood there thinking, I heard someone say, "Adam. Adam, did you hear what I said?"

"Yes, Ms. Brown," I said with a smile on my face.

Yes, I did just that, then she said, "What I'm about to say now is between you and I."

My face and feeling inside of me changed, just that fast. My world was taken away in a matter of seconds. Ms. Brown was telling me that my mom told the social work I was a troublemaker who never wanted to go to school and stole things from people. She said she had other children to worry about. If he can steal, he can take care of himself. As I was hearing these words, my body want dark. My thoughts were killing Ms. Brown for lying. How can this happen to me? What do I do now? I didn't shed a tear because there was nothing there, just darkness. She walked over to me and knelt down and said, "Adam, I'm sorry. I know your mom is missing out on something good."

Just then it was like life came into me. When she said that, tears ran down my face faster than I thought. I didn't know why or how was it, what she said, or that my mom didn't want me anymore and not seeing my brothers and sisters. She hugged me so hard. I was smiling like something I never smiled before, but I knew that was how I wanted to smile.

She said, "Adam, we will help you the best we can, but you have to let us help you."

In between my crying, I was nodding my head yes but not knowing that I was saying yes to Ms. Brown. She went on to say, "A social worker will talk to you soon, and we will go from there."

A couple days went by, and I was moved to another floor. These guys were kind of cool. They didn't fight that much, and they knew who to mess with. Some were sick. All I could do was think about what Ms. Brown said. I didn't eat, just picked at my food, stayed mad and angry, but wouldn't want anyone messing with me. Staff always said, "Adam, calm down," or "Do you need to sit in your room?" I was hurting, and I wanted everyone to hurt, but something would not allow me to hurt anyone or myself. The whole time, while I waited to go to court for breaking into homes and robbing and stealing cars, brand-new cars, the court wanted a background check on me because at that time I didn't know if your parents don't show for court or want you, you were awarded to the stat, and then they sent you where you needed to be. But what you have done also has something to do with where you end up. The staff was always talking to me about things in life, about moms, dads, what people do, what it takes to be good, always like they were my parents. Some I listened to and so you just knew they were full of will, you know. My turn came, and it was time to see the judge for the things I've done. I was scared. Things were running in my head back and forth, but what stood out the most was Mom not being here this time. I was all alone this time. I opened my eyes to allow the water in my eyes to come out, thinking, *How can I get out of this? It's morning soon, where's Mom? What will happen? What about what I've done to come here? Why did Mom move to city?*

I couldn't sleep. I walked around my little 10x10 cell quietly crying, praying to God, using him to help me. Not really knowing what or who he is. But I remember when we were young, Grandmom made us go to the Baptist Church, and Mom sent us to Pentecostal church. But I felt someone tapping me. "Adam, wake up. You have court today."

I looked at him, saying, "Yes, okay."

If you have court, they wake you up early then everybody else because you have to get dressed, eat, get moved somewhere else, then see your lawyer then split you up: felonies, runaways, whatever you've done. Some kids get in trouble a lot, so they call themselves a jail-house lawyer, and you talk about your case to them while you're waiting to see the judge. But you never believe them because they are still here or keep coming back. But I listen to them because, hey, you're locked up with them, and sometimes they say something good. I stood up, washed, put my clothes on, brushed my hair, opened my door to my room, and I looked around to see who was all going it was me and one other guy, but I didn't see him here before the staff walk over to me and said it's going to be okay today for you, I looked up at him with a small smile and nodded yes. I liked the morning staff. They were nice, not like second and third just you and the new guy have court. Come let's go eat breakfast. It was still dark outside, and people were asleep.

I didn't want to eat or see the judge. I could have been still asleep. Now I see why guys would say I'm going to court I'll see or talk to you latter. Then later come and you say, "Dude, where you been?"

He said, "Court."

"He'd been gone all day. It make you think they're doing something wrong to you."

As I'm walking and thinking this. I'm getting scared.

I say where, "Are we going, Mr. James? He turned and smiled to the dining hall for breakfast. I then said, "What about the other guys?"

He said, "They will eat later, the other staff will bring them."

I really was scared. Mr. James said, "It's okay. Come, Adam."

Well, it wasn't like I could turn back because every hall had a door (metal), and you needed a key. We walked up to the door leading to the dining room. We stopped. Mr. James knocked on the door. Where were his keys? Why was he knocking?

I said, "What's wrong?"

"Nothing," said Mr. James.

"Why are you knocking?" I said

"I don't have my keys right now."

The door opened. He let us come through, then said, "Good morning. You boys look like you're hungry this morning."

He was big and fat with a long beard like Santa and was nice. I've never seen him before, and plus I've never been up this early. He took us to eat, and Mr. James left while we were eating. I was watching Santa while he was drinking his coffee. I said to the other guy, "My name is Adam, but they call me Eastside."

He looked and said, "Kevin is my name."

"If Santa tries anything we will have to jump him."

Kevin laughed and said, "Who? Mr. Crawly?"

"Yes!" I said. "He's real nice. He let us stay up late sometimes when we have him on our dorm."

I looked at Kevin, then he went on to say, "I've been here for months now. I'm going to court."

I said, "I been here two and a half months."

Kevin said, "Was supposed to go to court last month but I got sick, so I couldn't."

I said, "What, you went home?"

Kevin laughed. "No, dummy, they put me in the sick unit until I got better."

"Hey, I'm not dumb," I said, mad.

"I know. I didn't mean it like that."

I said to Kevin, "Just don't say dumb, okay?"

"Ok," he said.

Just then I liked him. We talked some more while eating, came to find out that he had done some of the things I've done. He said he had been to DH four times. He was in for wrecking his dad's car into the neighbor's house. Mr. James came back with some papers and ask us were we ready to go. We said yes. Mr. James was telling us what was going to take place in the next hours and where we would be until we see the judge.

I asked, "Mr. James, do I have to go?"

He nodded and said yes.

"Don't worry, Adam, some staff wrote some things to the judge on your behalf. I'm sure you'll be okay."

Kevin said, "Yeah, Adam, you'll be fine."

I smiled and thought to myself, *Yeah, it'll be okay.*

We went into these rooms. Mr. James put me in one and Kevin on the other.

"Y'all will be here until your lawyer comes."

I said, "I don't have one."

Mr. James said, "The court will give you none."

Kevin said, "I hate him," then walked into his room. Then me. The door closed and locked. I wanted to know what Kevin meant.

So I said out the door, "Screw Kevin."

Kevin asked, "What do you mean by that?" He said, "My daddy is going to send his lawyer with my mom, and now I have to stay with my dad this summer."

I said, "That's not bad, at least you know you're getting out."

"Yeah," he said. Kevin then said, "Who you live with?"

"With my mom," I said.

"Will you get sad at what he just said?"

"No, that's not true. My mom don't want me."

Kevin and I said nothing until they called us and we both said good luck to each other. As we started walking toward the bench where you sat and waited, there was a kid in front of me, and he said, "What's up?" So did I. Then I ask him, "You know this judge?"

He said, "All I know is he is hard and sometimes nice. When the guys come from court they would say he was nice or she is a prick. Or I'm going to kill him, but you knew all the judges aren't nice."

I sat back and waited. I closed my eyes, leaned back. A tap on the shoulder. "Adam, come."

The boy was going out one door, and I was coming in through another. He looked at me and said, "I'm going home. Good luck."

I said, "Thanks."

He opened the door, walked me up to the front of the table, and said, "Have a seat."

I did. He walked away. I sat and looked at the man in front of me; I've never seen this before. A lady talking to the judge, him sitting up there, real high people in the courtroom talking, looking at you. Then I hear, "All parties for Adam Jones. I said parties on Adam Jones."

Then this lady walked up and two men. One came by me, and the other went over to the other table. The lady I've seen before, and the man I didn't know him. She said, "You might remember me, but I'm from children services, and this is your lawyer. We are here today about the things they said you did and to get you out of here.|

She went on to say that my mom couldn't come because they haven't heard from them or that she never called them back when they stopped by the home. "So now we need to help you go to a relative."

We sat down, then the lady stood up by the judge and started reading things off this paper, like I broke into a car lot, stole keys, money, cars. Then she said I was stealing out of stores and not going to school to help her around the house.

She also went on to say to the judge about what I did when I was five years old about stealing government mail and got sent to child care services for seven years. The judge wanted to know have I been in trouble before and then she started reading my pass. I didn't think they knew that I wasn't living in Columbus. As she was saying these things about me, all I could think about is where Mom is, why ain't she here. As I sat there looking into space, I could hear the lady next to me say something to the lawyer, but I couldn't move my head. I just kept looking at the judge and lady saying all this stuff. Just then the judge said to my lawyer if he would like to say something.

My lawyer went on to say, "Adam as a little boy moved to the city from a small town and got caught up with the wrong people."

The judge looked at me and said, "Is this true, Adam?"

I didn't know what to say because I was taught not to tell no matter what. I looked at the judge then my lawyer and then the lady. They nodded their head to me. When I looked at the judge I said yes with a shaky voice as if somebody was ready to kill me. Then some other lady stood up on the other side of me and read off about how long I had been locked up; how would I act while there? Then she went on to say, "We would like Adam kept in the court, so we can see why he keeps getting into trouble."

"This is not his first time." Now she was saying bad things to me and about me. That was when I put my head down, because I didn't know what was going on, and I didn't know these people. All I knew was that I was sorry, and I wanted Mom to come and get me. I looked back at the doors and benches to see if they were coming, but nothing. Just then she touched me and stood up and started talking. She was saying that I needed court help and said I came from a broken home. She had spoken to mom sometime back about her son, Adam. She stated that she had other kids, not just Adam, and she couldn't keep up with him. She also went on to say that children's services was working with the family. She also asked the court if they would send me to other family members. The judge asked her, "Do you have names, phone numbers?"

She said, "No, but we're working on it."

Then she turned to me and asked, "Do you know any family up here?"

I shook my head painfully, no. She sat down, and everybody was not talking, just writing on paper and looking at each other. The judge said okay in a strong voice. "Let's proceed."

He asked my lawyer and child services, "Is there something you would like to say before I speak to Adam's lawyer?"

He stood and said, "Adam should get a second chance. He's been here for four and a half months. One fight and staff say he's now a threat."

The lady stood and said, "Adam shouldn't be locked away but checked out, some counseling, and hopefully placed back home with family."

Then she touched me to stand. The judge said, "Would you like to say something?"

I looked at him and at everybody else. I looked at them scared, not knowing what to say. I turned around and said I was sorry, and tears ran down my face. Nobody move or said anything. I heard some clear their throat, and then I heard, "We find Adam Jones guilty of stealing, breaking and entering, and truancy from school. Vandalizing. The court will also note that Adam has been locked up four months and some days." Then he stopped talking.

But she touched my arm, and her lips said, "It's going to be okay, he is a fair judge. I sat there playing with my fingers, and they were wet from sweat. The judge asked me to stand, but I couldn't move. It was like I was stuck to the chair. She touched me. I stood and looked at the judge. He said, "Adam, you will be placed in the youth service and be evaluate and then placed where you can get some help." He also want on to say, "It's up to you when you get out. If you do what they say and show you can handle society, then you'll go home. Good day."

I stood their looking at them. Everybody was picking up their papers. I looked at the lawyer and the lady and asked, "Am I going home?"

She looked at me then the lawyer and then me and said, "I'm afraid not there going to ___ you somewhere else."

Then she said, "Somebody will be talking to you soon, hang in there."

The guard came over to me and said, "Please, let's go."

As I walked with the guard, I looked at the people in the courtroom to see if I would see Mom. With tears in my eyes. I couldn't let these people see me crying. I wiped my face, stood up strong, and walked. He led me to this holding room and said, "Just sit here, I'll be back for you."

Then he shut the door and looked into the screen window. "Will you be okay?"

I looked back with tears in my eyes and said yes. "But what happened?"

He said, "They will explain it to you soon."

As I heard the guard walk away, I sat down on the cement block, put my head in my hands, trying to figure this all out. Replaying what just happened. What did he mean youth commission? Where are they going to send me? And for how long? I just got used to this place. I couldn't think no more. I started crying, getting madder at Mom for not coming. Why did she leave me here like this? She didn't love me anymore. I sat there for a moment then I yelled real loud for Mom. But the only thing that happened was that the guard came. "Guys!" he was yelling. "Say, what's wrong?" He was looking out the door screens. He opened the door and came in and knelt down. "What's wrong, Adam?"

My nose runny, my eyes filled with tears. I looked up at this black light-skinned man and said, "My mom don't love me."

He put his hand on my back and said, "Yes, she does. Please come with me."

We walked into the elevator. The door closed. He said, "I'm just going to take you back. You don't need to sit down here, it's been a long morning for you. I'm going to tell the staff to leave you alone for a while. I'll stop by before my shift is up to see how you're doing. Now the longer you're locked up, you can't help but know guards, staff, people, judges, and they learn you. Everybody liked me, some people didn't. Bullies didn't like me or mean people with nasty attitudes and white guys who hate blacks."

When I got back to the dorm, everybody came up to me and said, "What happened? You going home?"

The guard backed them away and said, "He'll talk to y'all later. Let him by right now."

One of my buddies walked by me and said, "You'll be okay. I'll talk to you later," and gave me a bag of chips. We went to the front office and walked in. I sat. They talked. One of the staff said, "Come, Adam, let's get you some rest before lunch."

I said okay because I just wanted to be alone. I went to my room. He unlocked it. I went in and put the pillow over my head, so I couldn't hear the guys out there watching TV shows before lunch, like Bob Barker from *The Price Is Right*, and also so they wouldn't hear me crying. I don't know how long I was asleep, but the door opened. I jumped up like somebody was about to hurt me. One of the staff said, "Wash your face and hands, time for lunch."

I nodded and said, "Okay, here I come." After I washed my face, I went out. The guys looked back at me. Some smiled, some gave me the peace sign to let me know we were cool. We started walking down the hall. They were talking, singing like we always did. Going to lunch, but today I didn't want to sing or laugh. Just leave me alone. I didn't even want to eat today. Cheeseburger and fries are my favorite, but not today. We get our trays and sit down at our tables with our boys who we ride with, but I walked past my boys and set the table with nobody at all. They looked at me and said, "What, you better than us now?"

I looked and walked on and sat down. The staff said, "Leave him alone. That right, Adam?"

I looked over my shoulder with my back to everybody, and I guess two days went by, and the guys who stayed in my room quit going to the gym; staff was worried about me. They knew what was going on with me but nobody else. Staff would keep an eye on guys who came back from court with bad news; some guys would hurt themselves, so they would send them to the hospital or not get sent away, but it didn't matter. Because I had a cast on my leg they locked me up. My boys kept sliding notes under my door.

"What happened, talk to us. Come to gym, or dinner."

But I would ball it up. And look out the window to the street. Trying to figure out how to get out of here. What if I cut myself? What if I hit somebody? What can I do now? Was I going to see Mom? My sisters and brother? Why am I always getting into trouble? How come I couldn't be like him or Lorri? Why me? Mom showed me these things in life; she was not going to stick by me. Who was the blame for this? Was it me, Mom, Dad, Surgest, who? As days went by, I didn't hear from Mom or the lawyer. I started thinking they lied to me like Mom did. The more I thought about this, the more I got mad. It was Friday, and my buddy was going to court. "I'll see you later, I have court," he said.

I looked at him and said nothing. They started walking down toward the door. I said, "I hope you get out."

He turned and smiled and waved to me. I really didn't mean it because I didn't go home. So I didn't want anybody to go home. Our day went by like clockwork: TV, playing cards, lying about what we did on the street. One of the guys I knew said, "What are they going to do with you?"

I looked at him. His boy hit him. "Don't say that. Adam hasn't talked in days about that."

I said, "I will when our boys come back from court."

They laughed and said, "Man, we're glad. We thought you were going to do something stupid."

I said, "It's not over yet."

They looked and said, "Man, quit playing."

I said, "I'm not."

We went to lunch, and my boy didn't come back from court yet. I said over lunch to my boys, "Will you guys leave next week, and I'll still be here?"

They said, "Man, you're going home."

I just looked and said nothing. My boy was telling us what he was going to do when he'd get home, then my dude said he was going to hit his dad and eat some good food. We liked him because he was tall and big. Always telling people that he would bite your head off and flush it down the toilet. And always taking things from the white guys. If they were watching TV he would turn the channel then ask them was you watching that they would say no because they were scared of him. But we would say, "Yeah, man, I was watching. Then he would say, "I wasn't talking to you with a mean face," and we would laugh at him; we knew it made him mad. We didn't have a lot of time to watch TV after lunch because we would have chores, and two thirty count time, which meant you'd be in your room until three thirty count. Then we would come out for mail, showers, write letters, then dinner at 5:00 p.m. Man, I hated not going outside. Or seeing my friends. I looked in my boy's room, but he still wasn't there yet. So I asked my boy, have they come back?"

He was like, "Man, you know they take all day to bring you back."

I didn't know why I was worried about him because he was in for stealing and driving without a license, so they weren't going to let him go and can hang out some more till it was time for me to leave. Count time, we all got up and went to our rooms and shut the door so they could count us. I was lying on my bed, looking at the ceiling, thinking about what I was going to do when I got out. Or where would I be and how dead would I be. Would I see Mom? *Do they miss me?* I wondered. Where is the lawyer at? I've been here for some time now, and no one has seen me or written me. When they said, "Okay, mail time," everybody would get up and go to the office, but I wouldn't because nobody has written me since I'd been here. Why start now? Some days I would go to my room when people got mail. Everybody knew how I felt. Some would say Mom said hi or my sis said what's up. But they wanted me to feel like they felt.

I got up and asked one of the staff where the court was. He said they'd be back before dinner.

"Okay," I said.

One of the staff said, "Are you doing better?"

I said, "Yes, but I still want to see my mom."

He said, "I know, I wish I could help."

"Me too," I said. I'll never forget the day my boy left. He came back from court, smiling, saying real loud, "I'm going home to, smoke."

Guys were patting him on the back, saying, "Yeah, all right. I'll hit you up when I get out."

I was sitting at the table, acting like I didn't hear them. My boys got up and want to shake his hand and give him five. I knew what was next. My dude would leave the station real soon, then he was gone. You don't see them until they get in trouble again. He walked over to me and said, "I'm sorry we couldn't talk, but whatever you need, hit me up.

I looked at him and got bad news. He walked over to the station, so the staff would let him get his stuff then got ready to go. If someone gave you all their stuff that meant you were cool, and if somebody left you all their stuff and they were the boss, people had to do for you like they did for him. And that was how it was happening. My boy left and gave me power to be whoever I wanted to be, besides the kid who nobody cared about. *Knock, knock* is what I heard at the door. I opened my cell door.

"It was my dude," he said. The staff said he could talk to me before he left.

I looked at him with a smile on my face and said, "Man, it's count time. You got that much pull?"

He smiled and said, "When you got it you got it. By the way, I'm leaving now, so here are some things for you and what I do on Fridays with the guys."

I said, "Yeah."

It was make a list of goodies and people who got visited would bring it back—money, dope, food, candy, clothes, etc. etc.

I looked at him and said, "No, man, I can't do this, it ain't me."

He shoved his hand out there, and I shook it with my right hand, and I felt something in my hand. He looked at me and said, this is my book keep. And use it. The boys told me your mom didn't come to court. That's why you can do this. What have you got to lose except what guys say. You know, the boys got your front.

Then we slapped a high five, and he turned and walked out the door. I sat on the bed and thought to myself, *Why am I sad that my boy is going home?* Was it because I couldn't or was just mad because my dude left? *What am I going to do now?* I thought.

As I served the rest of my time, I remembered that I still had this little black book. I kept everybody's name in it that owed me (clout card). It went all the way back to my juvenile time. This little black book was my way to live good when I got out. Debt that people owed me. Things I have done to help people out who was scared to stay alive in jail. Now I was going before the parole board in nineteen days, and this was 1987, November 3, and tomorrow was my birthday. As days went by, I saw some guys who didn't care too much about me. They wanted me to start a fight with them, and that wouldn't look good for me. I've stopped selling drugs and let my friend have my store. I didn't want to give that away; it brought good money to me. I sold coffee, cookies, soap, cigarettes, pop. I give you items until you went to the store, and you gave me two back of what I gave you. So I gave it away because you could get into trouble. It was called extortion, making somebody give you back more than what you gave them with force. As I slept, and days were getting close for me to see the parole board. I couldn't sleep. People were talking s—t to me because they knew I had a date with the parole board. I just kept thinking to myself at bedtime, *Where are you going? It's been years since you've talked or seen your family and friends.* I was scared. I've been here four and a half years, not worried about nothing. This is my world.

I built it myself. How to have power when you came home. But I knew deep inside me I was scared. I didn't know where my mom lived. I have not seen her or talked to her. Would she want me or not? Today is November 10. They were moving me because I was going to the parole board. So you have to be separated from the population and moved over to another wing where they got paroled or they were going to be paroled. It was some new shit than what you see on the other side of the same wall. I'd sit here with those new guys about eight to ten days until it was time to see the parole board. I've never seen any of these guys since I've been down. Now, I cannot say or tell what I have done to live in here, nor let people know. Some used it to get out, make them look good. I've seen people make a deal. I guess you see what I'm trying to say. I'm just being cool now, gambling, laughing, and eating. Talking is what we do in lock down. Some people talked about what they would say. Some said they didn't think they would get out. There were those that had their date when they were going home, and they would speak to us and give us hope, and some would tell the truth to us. Like if you had been locked up for murder, rape, etc., etc. No, you don't go home. We were locked up because they said I was a threat to them. The food we ate here was different from what we were eating on the other side of the wall. After eating cookies, cakes, breads, and lots of coffee, man, this food was good. I never (not too much) ate the food while I was locked down.

Now my mind was going around very fast. It seemed like the days were coming fast. I started thinking about what I was going to do. How my mom was going to treat me when I came home. Would they smile or give me a big hug? Give me a party? I heard someone call my name, but I was numb from thinking about my family.

Finlay someone shook me. I jumped up and said, what the hell. And the guy looked at me and said, "Sorry, but it's dinner."

I nodded at him. I stood in line, waiting for my meal. I said to myself, "What the fuck, Adam, you're not getting out. They only let people loose who come back."

So I shook the thought off about going home to whom. Where do they live? Is my mom still alive? I stood up straight in line, put my mean face on, and said out loud, "I'll go see the parole board tomorrow. I'm ready to do the rest of my time if that's what they want me to do."

Some guys looked at me, some patted me on the back, and others shook their heads. But they didn't know what I did. No one come to see me, write me, nothing. The whole time I was locked down.

I came too far to get broken down. I had to stay strong for these people in the morning. It was 6:00 p.m. I was watching the news to get my mind off the parole and what they were going to do with me.

I started thinking about all the stuff I had been doing since I got here in my security. And it was not looking good—two fights, a stabbing, gambling, got caught smoking pot. Bullying a guy for his money.

I heard: "Hey, do you want to play spades?" Then he said it again. "Well, do you or not?"

I turned and said to him, "Not really."

He said, "It'll get your mind off what you're thinking about."

"We've all been there and are seeing each other too in the morning." I walked over to the table and sat down and said, "I'm not dealing." Everyone laughed.

Today was the big day. We were up at 5:30 a.m. There were eight of us going for parole, and rumor has it that they were only letting two or three people go. I was thinking what my odds were.

I heard someone say, "Number 131-060, step out of your cell."

I didn't move. Then I heard him again, "Number 131-060, step out of your cell."

I went out and looked at the guard and said, "Yes, sir."

"Get in line, you're going to breakfast then see the board."

My heart started pounding, and my palms were wet. As the guard called more names, I felt sick, like I was going to pass out. I wiped my hands and face, stood still, until it was time to walk. We sat at the table; nobody was talking. Some were eating, and some were just sitting there, thinking about what was going to happen. This is the time where it can break you either way if you stayed or went home. I've seen people get paroled and come back to the block, get into a big fight, and end up losing their walking papers. Some were scared to go home; some didn't have a place to go. We were on our way down the hall to these chairs outside this door, and there was a light that told you when to come in. Now this was the only time you'd hear your name because it was by alphabetical order, by last name. When the light come on, the guard said, "Inmate Brown."

One guy went in, and I was two people behind him. I looked at my left and said to the guy, "Good luck."

And he said, "You too."

Wow, it was hot in here, my head was wet, and my palms were sweating. I was next. I was scared. I didn't want to go in. I just wanted to go back to bed.

"Jones." he said. I couldn't move.

My name is inmate Jones now. I stood up, walked to the door, and looked back as I grabbed the doorknob and saw one of the guys give me thumbs-up, and I turned and walked in.

ABOUT THE AUTHOR

The author was born in 1964, at a time when kids were seen and not heard. He knew as he was growing up that he wanted to help troubled kids because he was also one troubled kid. He is now fifty-three years old and a proud father of six children whose ages range from ten to twenty eight years old. For the past fifteen years he has worked for a local labor union as a skilled construction worker. He has always had a passion for books and writing. His goal is that this book will help others and touch the lives of those who read it.

CPSIA information can be obtained
at www.ICGtesting.com
Printed in the USA
BVHW031946310821
615711BV00007B/153